My Business
My Mission

Stories from around the world told by

DOUG SEEBECK | TIMOTHY STONER

Foreword by Richard M. DeVos, co-founder of Amway Corporation

Partners Worldwide
Grand Rapids, Michigan

Cover photo by Sarah Patty
Cover design by Andrea MacLurg

Library of Congress Cataloging in Publication Data
Seebeck, Doug.
My business, my mission : fighting poverty through partnerships: stories from around the world / told by Doug Seebeck and Timothy Stoner; foreword by Richard M. DeVos.
    p. cm.
ISBN 978-1-59255-500-0 (alk. paper)
1. Partnership. 2. Poverty—International cooperation. I. Stoner, Timothy.
II. Title.
HD69.S8.S435 2009
362.5'5765092—dc22

2009010347

10 9 8 7 6 5 4 3 2 1

Contents

120910

Foreword

BY RICHARD M. DEVOS

his book will challenge and change you. If you equate business owners or entrepreneurs with greed and self-interest, you will be surprised. If you are a Christian who believes a wealthy person is incapable of being a disciple of Jesus Christ, you will be enlightened. If you are convinced the rich care nothing for the poor and cannot play a significant role in helping overcome world poverty, this book will be a revelation.

Above all, if you are a successful businessperson who has never considered that your ability to run a business is a talent God has given you to help do his will on earth as in heaven, you may discover in this book a true calling.

I was flattered and excited when Doug Seebeck asked me a few years ago to be a mentor in helping achieve his ambitious vision for Partners Worldwide. I admired his confidence and enthusiasm and the fact that his vision was so big.

As the co-founder of Amway, I shared the same passion for big dreams, which helped propel Amway from its start in a couple of home basements to a global corporation. I also shared Doug's belief in partnership. My lifelong business partner and friend, Jay Van Andel, and I built a business that relied on groups of people supporting each other. Doug was and is passionate about providing people a hand up to help themselves and others through partnership. He believes that those who are less fortunate than he or I possess equal potential and must be given the chance to realize it. This was consistent with my business philosophy of "people helping people to help themselves."

Doug was not asking me first for funding, but to be his mentor. He was looking to tap a businessman's advice on using real-world business principles for a heavenly cause. It was a revolutionary idea to take the God-given talents of businesspeople and harness them for partnership in kingdom purposes.

Doug initially approached me after reading my book *Compassionate Capitalism*. I gave my book this title because I knew most people would be taken aback by thinking that a capitalist could have compassion. I wanted people to realize how the talents and resources of the rich are vital to helping encourage the talents and tap the resources of the poor. People living in poverty cannot by themselves lift others out of poverty. Capitalists are challenged by the biblical command that of those to whom much is given, much is expected. In my experience, successful businesspeople respond in amazing ways.

At the core of Doug's vision is a strong faith in God with a belief that God blesses each person with special talents to help others. That includes using the talents of successful businesspeople—not simply to offer charitable contributions, but to get personally involved. Through the mission of Partners Worldwide, Doug hopes to encourage businesspeople everywhere to put all their entrepreneurial, organizational, and leadership skills to work to make a meaningful difference in the lives of people who want to work to build better lives for themselves, their families, and their communities. You will find many examples of this vision in the stories of the incredible people in this book.

I have always had a deep desire to reflect God and impact his kingdom in my daily work of business. My personal passion for evangelism takes advantage of my position as a businessperson to share my faith. Many years ago, when I was about to address a large group of businesspeople, I was introduced with a list of achievements and accolades. I acknowledged the glowing introduction but told the crowd that they needed to know who I really am: "A sinner saved by grace." God has given each of us talents and created each person for a purpose so that we can be used for a heavenly cause.

But, in a way, that was never quite enough. Connecting with the work of Doug Seebeck and Partners Worldwide has been an encouragement to me personally. I too shared experiences similar to those of Milt Kuyers and John Vander Ploeg, whose stories are told in this book. I longed to have a place to make significant spiritual contributions in and through the marketplace. Partners Worldwide now provides a vehicle for business men and women to do just that.

Partners Worldwide is also a living testament to all that I believe about the ability of people to use God's gifts to help people to help themselves. Poverty is not an affliction but a condition that can be overcome. Many of the same principles that have helped me in business—unlimited potential, free enterprise, an upward look, human dignity, persistence, family, freedom, and faith—are vital to lifting people out of poverty. That is why I was inspired by Doug's vision to recruit a million business-people to partner with the world's poor by mentoring them and working together to create the capacity to care for themselves, their families, and their communities.

If you are successful through your talents for business, I challenge you to act on the lessons you will learn in this book. I challenge churches and nonprofits to see businesspeople as more than check writers and financial advisors and to personally engage their donors to maximize their business skills beyond their ability to offer financial support. Finally, I would ask everyone with the means to help the less fortunate to partner with Partners Worldwide.

Enjoy this book. I know you will be inspired and changed in profound ways.

About This Book

BY DOUG SEEBECK

This book is about a movement that is changing the lives of tens of thousands of people in some of the most impoverished nations on earth. It is also transforming businesspeople in North America by exposing them to a paradigm that is—frankly—revolutionary. It is happening as their eyes and hearts are being opened to the amazing potential to serve Christ by using their business skills in the marketplace.

Entrepreneurs who see their business as their mission (people we sometimes like to call "missioneurs") recognize that they have been called *into* mission—not *out of* business. Whereas old paradigms encourage businesspeople to believe they are unsuited for ministry, they now see that God can use them as businesspeople for vital and unique kingdom work.

Their mission is simple: to expand business, create wealth, and provide jobs for the poor in Christ's name. Our vision statement at Partners Worldwide makes it clear: "Business as ministry for a world without poverty." What we want to see is the kingdom of God being manifest on earth: where the rich and the poor are liberated from the shackles that bind them to become lovers of God and agents of his blessing to others.

Through our global network, we link North American businesspeople with high-impact entrepreneurs in Africa, Asia, and Latin America. Partnering together, they create innovative solutions for economic growth that restore hope and dignity to people around the world.

By walking alongside emerging entrepreneurs in developing countries we discover new ways to create jobs, support families, and eliminate poverty. Local business groups and training centers continue these efforts, bringing sustainable change to whole business communities. But what drives us is the commitment to raise up agents of reconciliation who follow Christ by laying down their lives as he did for the reconciliation of the world: economic, social, and spiritual transformation.

In these pages you will read about some of these agents of reconciliation—remarkable people who have seen and tasted that the gospel is good news to the poor—as well as to the rich. Their stories are so powerful I can promise you this: when you are finished reading, not only will your life be changed, you will be challenged to join them and become a world-changer.

As I understood very clearly when my daughter and I were almost killed in a car accident in March 2001, our lives are not our own—we are bought with a great price. We are to bring glory to God by serving others. This is the great discovery and the great adventure you will be introduced to through the lives of businesspeople devoted to Christ's mission of reconciliation.

Why This Book?

First, let me explain how this book came about. For many years I was strongly opposed to the whole idea. What made me begin to think seriously about it was a conversation with Dr. Ken Eldred, a well-known venture capitalist. We were in his southern California office, discussing business ministry models, when he suddenly asked, "Have you written this stuff down? I'd like to include what you're sharing in the new book I'm writing, *God Is at Work*." I glibly dismissed his suggestion with my standard response, "People who write about it probably aren't doing it. We're practitioners."

Then in June 2006, Phyllis Hendry, the CEO of Lead Like Jesus, spoke at Partners Worldwide's International Business Conference. She was touched by the people she met and asked how she could get involved with Partners Worldwide. She then challenged my prejudice by telling me that if we were serious about our vision we needed to publish our story.

I was convinced that she was right, and I began to pray about it. About a year later, God led me to Timothy Stoner. His wife, Patty, was directing the discipleship program at The Potter's House, the inner-city Christian school my daughter, Jember, attends. As part of the program, Jember and most of the middle school children had memorized the entire book of James. At the celebration honoring their hard work I met Tim, a lawyer who had just returned from a trip to Uganda. Through Orphan Justice Mission, a nonprofit Tim helped establish, a team of businesspeople were providing food and education for more than 450 children, most of whom were AIDS orphans. We talked about how to sustain this ministry through business and entrepreneurial ventures in the Rakai district in southern Uganda.

During our conversation I discovered Tim is a writer. He was raised overseas, so I knew that he could gather the experiences of our international partners with respect and objectivity. He also had three years of seminary education before attending law school. This gave him the background in the church and theology that I felt was necessary. More important, he is totally surrendered to Jesus Christ.

After reading the manuscript of Tim's book *The God Who Smokes* (NavPress 2008), I asked him if he would visit our international business affiliates and North American teams and collect their stories. He agreed. When I told him we had to complete this project in six months, he swallowed hard and invoked the words from Mel Gibson's character in the film *The Patriot*: "Lord, make me fast, and Lord, make me accurate."

Since then we have learned much as we've listened to our partnership members. Our hope is that as you read their stories of struggle and pain, vision and astonishing tenacity, their slow but steady growth, and, in some cases, exceptional success, you will not only learn but be challenged.

It is our firm belief that you have been called to business "for such a time as this." Our prayer is that you will be motivated to take your place, fulfill your calling, and join this new movement of missionary/entrepreneurs who recognize that they have been blessed with business skills to be a blessing to their communities and to the nations of the earth, for Jesus' sake.

Michelle Jahnke

"In order for us to end poverty, we must connect the rich and the poor directly."

Partners Worldwide

The Vision

BY DOUG SEEBECK

I n 1976 I was a college sophomore working toward a degree in agronomy. In my first agricultural economics class I encountered the "Malthusian theory," which predicted that since world population grows exponentially and food production grows linearly, there would be massive starvation on our planet by the year 2025.

That hit me hard—2025 was within my lifetime! I just couldn't accept it. I didn't believe that Malthus understood the inherent creativity of imagebearers of God, nor the cosmic significance of Christ's death and resurrection. Two years later I graduated from Washington State University and started a career in agribusiness. I had a great job, which I jumped into with passion. But God had a plan to shake me out of my comfort zone.

Within the month I heard about an urgent need for an agronomist to serve with our church's relief and development agency. Despite being very happy with my work, I couldn't shake the call. I met with officials of the Christian Reformed World Relief Committee (CRWRC). They wanted me to go to Bangladesh, a country I knew nothing about. I rationalized, agonized, and argued with God. But in the end I accepted a three-year assignment to help Bengali farmers increase their production. Though I was terrified, I also felt deeply affirmed. I could barely believe that God would call a young farm boy to go across the world to do something reserved for the more "spiritual" missionaries.

Access to the Pond

At the time, Bangladesh's 100 million people were crammed into a land mass the size of Wisconsin. Food was scarce and people were chronically malnourished.

Everywhere I went, it seemed, beggars were pleading for money. I began to see why the Malthusian theory was, superficially at least, so compelling.

But I was also impressed by the skills of the Bengali farmers. With a little assistance and access to hybrid seeds and fertilizer (and water during the dry season) they could nearly equal the rice yield per unit of land of their Japanese or North American counterparts. I came to see that what they lacked was not *ability* but *acreage*. Most of the microfarmers in the program owned about half an acre to feed an average of seven people. At that time, less than 10% of the population owned more than half the land while almost half of the population was landless, working as serfs to increase the wealth of the large landowners.

I found myself protesting the old development cliché that says, "Give a man a fish, and you will feed him for day, but teach a man to fish and he will eat for a lifetime." "No!" I thought, "These people know how to fish. They just don't have access to the pond!"

I became more passionate about working for justice, and went at the task of improving the situation with a vengeance. As I neared the end of my three-year stay, we had established 14 field offices with more than 70 agricultural staff. We were working with more than 3,500 small farmers who were now capable of feeding their families.

By 1981 I felt satisfied that I had fulfilled my mission and worked myself out of a job. I began preparing to turn over my position to my close friend and Bengali counterpart, Abdus Salaam.

> My friend had offered me the key to releasing thousands of entrepreneurs into significant kingdom ministry and rescuing tens of thousands of people from poverty.

I hated to say goodbye to him. We had become as close as brothers, and we grieved to think we might never see each other again. In one of our final conversations, through tears, Abdus made a profound statement: "Doug, *bhai* (brother), I think we have been doing this poverty thing all wrong." I was taken aback by this unexpected indictment.

Abdus went on, "If we are ever going to solve the problem of very poor Bangladeshi farmers in this country, the rich Bengalis must get involved. We need to get them to care about the poor people in our country so that it becomes *their* concern and *their* problem, not the NGOs or *bideshis* from America." (NGO is an acronym for non-governmental organization. It's the equivalent of the North American term "nonprofit." *Bideshi* is the Bengali word for someone from another country.)

I heard what Abdus said, but it would take almost 10 years before I realized that my friend had offered me the key to releasing thousands of entrepreneurs into significant kingdom ministry and rescuing tens of thousands of people from poverty.

A New Partnership

As I contemplated life after Bangladesh, I talked to the Lord about it. "Lord," I said, "I think I am pretty good at this international crosscultural stuff, and I think I can do more of it." (I loved the Bengali way of life. I ate the spicy food with my hands. I slept on a hard 2-inch-thick mattress. I talked and even dreamed in Bangla.) "But," I told God, "I need a partner. If you will give me someone crazy enough to go to these kinds of places, I will spend my life working to end hunger and poverty, if that's what you want me to do."

Back in the States, I felt convicted about my attempt to strike a bargain with God. I told him that I would obey his call without conditions. The next Sunday, while attending my first service at Madison Square Church in Grand Rapids, Michigan, I was irresistibly drawn to a beautiful young woman.

Pastor Dave Beelen introduced her to the congregation. She was a nurse on her way to serve the poor in Harlem, New York. Her name was Gail Hoekstra. Pastor Dave informed us that she needed to find an apartment in the city. I had just been to New York a few months before to talk to donors about my work in Bangladesh. I battled with my altruistic and romantic motives. I decided I had to do the right thing and help this young missionary out, so I gave her the name of some people to contact about New York apartments.

She went to Harlem, but things didn't end there. Exactly five months later, Gail and I were married. We had barely finished our honeymoon when the Lord opened the doors for us to work with Ugandan refugees. Eight months later all our belongings were packed into four bags and we arrived in Kenya as the first field staff for CRWRC in East Africa.

We lived in Nairobi for just over a year, during which we traveled and developed program strategies in Sudan, Uganda, and Kenya. By that time it was clear that despite the instability caused by the coup that toppled Idi Amin and the ensuing civil war in its wake, we would be more effective living in Uganda.

What stands out about our arrival in Uganda is the fear and tension. It was like a toxic cloud—you could almost smell it. There were 26 roadblocks on the 40-kilometer road between the Entebbe airport and Kampala. They were all manned by drunken soldiers. Amin's ouster had left a dangerous leadership vacuum, and it was a frightening and chaotic time to be in that country. The army would impose martial law at night and then the killings would begin. During the years we lived there, approximately 500,000 people were murdered.

We spent the next 14 years initiating and managing community development programs, first in Uganda and then in nine other countries in eastern and southern Africa. These were unbelievably great times. We grew ministry partnerships, and our own family grew to five members. We used to joke that we would add a new

The Seebeck family in 1996

country and a new child every two years. Our first two biological children, Lucas and Maisha, were born in Uganda during the brutal civil war that followed the coup that ended Amin's reign of terror.

It all came together for me in a slum just outside Nairobi during a brief conversation that opened my heart.

On the night of February 6, 1986, Gail was in the clinic holding newborn Lucas when gunshots rang out around Nysambya Hospital. Gail hid under a bed for protection, but then saw that the mosquito netting covering the bed did not reach to the concrete floor. Fearful of contracting malaria, she crawled back into bed, cradling our son in her shaking arms.

Twenty months later Maisha was born, but this time Gail declined the overnight stay and came straight home. That evening, tracers screamed across the valley and over our house nestled among the hills of Kampala. We moved the cribs into a windowless hallway and away from danger. The next morning I discovered the army had only been celebrating the capture of rebel Alice Lakwena.

Our last three children, Markos Abdissa ("the chosen one" in Oromo), Jordana Tamirnesh ("the miracle" in Amharic), and Jember Lishan ("the sunrise" in Amharic), were adopted from Ethiopia during the civil war under the Mengistu regime, a dark period during which more than 100,000 children were orphaned.

My Conversion

In the spring of 1992, John DeHaan, the executive director of CRWRC, arrived with a group of U.S. business owners on a "discovery trip" to Kenya. I have to admit that at first I was not thrilled to have them touring our mission territory. I had seen wealthy Americans come and go with big ideas and big plans before. I had seen firsthand the damage caused by confident Westerners with good intentions but little crosscultural experience and sensitivity.

The more time we spent together, however, the more I realized that these visitors were different than many who had preceded them. They weren't just here on a jaunt to visit the world-famous Masai Mara game reserve and take a little "missions" detour to the slums. They seemed to be seriously committed to finding out how they could help with the desperate social and economic problems. I began to soften toward them, especially when I witnessed how impacted they were by the pain and the suffering all around them.

It all came together for me in a slum just outside Nairobi during a brief conversation that opened my heart and eventually helped launch Partners Worldwide.

John Vander Ploeg, one of the businessmen on the trip, pulled me aside in front of a dilapidated tea kiosk. He said, "Doug, here's the thing. You are affirmed in the church because of your role as a missionary. You're at the top of the ladder. Pastors are on the next rung. Then come the teachers, doctors, nurses, social workers, even farmers. But the church keeps successful businesspeople at arm's length. It's like there's a suspicion that we must have done something underhanded to get our wealth. But we are still constantly being asked to give money to the church! We are not allowed to sit around the ministry table and plan with you about how things will be done. Our role is to wait outside in the foyer and be told how much to write the check for."

I could tell this had bothered John for a long time. "This is my bottom-line question," he continued. "Is there a way for businesspeople to become personally involved and use their management expertise, their leadership, and their financial and business skills to become part of the solution to ending poverty, instead of being seen as part of the problem?"

> "Is there a way for businesspeople to become personally involved and use their business skills to become part of the solution to ending poverty, instead of being seen as part of the problem?"

That one question pierced me and crystallized some very important issues: Abdus's exhortation to connect the rich with the poor; the importance of feeling affirmed in the body of Christ; the need for self-sustaining ministries, and the necessity of freeing the poor from dependence on charity. It also reinforced the significance of what Milt Kuyers had said to me a few days earlier.

That conversation took place at a lodge in the Tsavo Game Reserve after a long day visiting the work of the Mangalete Community Development Organization. As we talked, Milt surprised me with these insightful words: "Doug, I know that my job as a Christian is to proclaim the good news of Jesus Christ. I am to provide the cup of cold water, do justice, and love mercy every day. I am responsible to help the poor in Milwaukee and in Kenya too. But right now I give you my money and you do that job for me. I need you to help me. Please teach me what I need to know. Help make the connections for me, and then let *me* help the poor, person to person!"

As I thought over this earnest request, along with John Vander Ploeg's question, my Bengali friend's comments years earlier seemed to thunder in my ears: "In order for us to end poverty, we must connect the rich and the poor directly."

That was it! That moment was what I call my "conversion."

Partners for Christian Development, now Partners Worldwide, was officially born in 1994. The concept was simple. Our organization would help successful businesspeople in North America partner with entrepreneurs in the developing world for economic development.

Dr. Dennis (Denny) Hoekstra and his wife, Jeni, came to Kenya the next year as the first active volunteer members of our fledgling organization. Denny had just stepped down as the executive director of The Barnabas Foundation, where he helped over 3,000 families establish estate plans that channeled significant resources to Christian ministry.

One conversation especially helped define my thinking. I was explaining the importance of "sustainability" in our development efforts. This concept had been talked about for several years by those of us in international development, and now Denny was getting a little frustrated. With a wicked little grin on his face, he said, "I hear much talk among NGOs about this thing called 'sustainability.' But I'm starting to think that it's a little like ghosts—you hear a lot about them, but no one has ever actually seen one." It was funny and it stung too, because it was true. We were all discussing sustainability at length, but no one had the slightest idea how to pull it off. We all had clearly established deadlines to phase out funding with local organizations, but no one I knew had ever succeeded. This underscored the importance of for-profit enterprises as a key solution to ending poverty.

Denny was the one who helped convince me to leave the continent my family and I had grown to love and return to the U.S. to put some operational wheels under the vision. In the summer of 1996, our family reluctantly moved to Grand Rapids, Michigan, leaving behind precious relationships, broad networks, and solid partnerships along the eastern flank of that great continent.

As you'll read in the next chapter, we began our work in Kenya. But since then, the partnership model has spread to 20 other countries around the world.

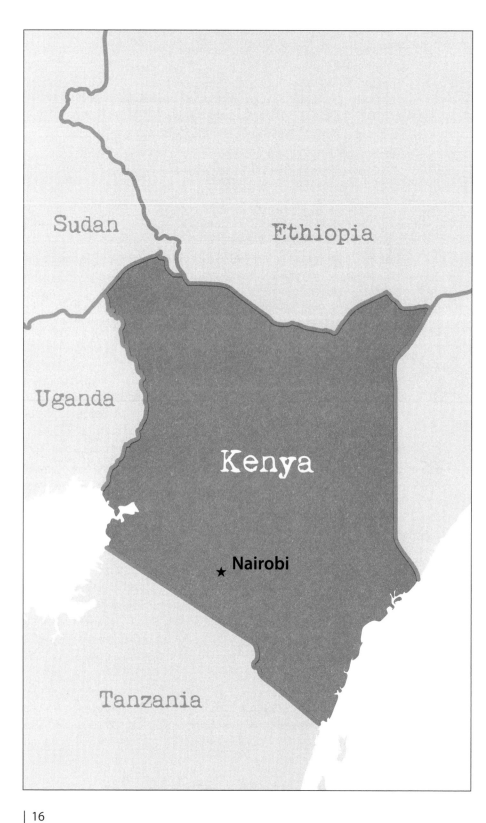

Kenya

The Context

BY DOUG SEEBECK

Eighteen years in the developing world had taught me that one of the first obstacles to breaking the cycle of poverty is in the mind. Before the exodus out of economic bondage can begin, a powerful cultural lie needs to be exposed and renounced: that it is God's will for the poor to be poor. That lie crushes the hope that sparks initiative, encourages risk, and allows people to move from survival to prosperity. Mental poverty helps ensure economic poverty. What I did not expect upon my return to the United States was the discovery that the rich were also being held hostage by beliefs that were equally false and just as oppressive.

This mental poverty was manifested in comments I heard repeated scores of times: "When I sell my business, I am going to go into ministry," or "My job is to make as much money as I can in order to fund good ministries." These comments were based on the lie that businesspeople can not engage in significant work for the kingdom through business. The rich had accepted a lie that hindered them from fulfilling their calling as agents of transformation, robbing them of realizing their full potential. Both the rich and the poor needed to have lies exposed and faith aroused.

We organized our first conference, titled "Business '97, An Outstanding Christian Calling!" Its message affirmed that God delights in businesspeople and has given them a trust to fulfill his purposes and bring about his will on earth. As a businessperson you have a special creative capacity that is rare, and you don't have to be a church employee to do real ministry. You have a kingdom calling in business, and God wants your company to be a place of ministry.

I returned to Kenya that same year, but this time went with a large group of U.S. Partners. These "marketplace missionaries" met with their business peers in Nairobi to discuss how they could work together to fight poverty in that beautiful country.

The Kenya Investment Trust (KIT) was created to form partnerships with small, medium, and large enterprises for the purpose of creating sustainable jobs. The binational group also identified specific strategies to tackle unemployment rates that exceeded 50%. They would focus on mentoring, training, and coaching; access to affordable capital and appropriate technology; and advocacy for free and fair trade to create a level economic playing field. Finally, they would form business associations, trusts, and cooperatives to provide the legal entities and organizational infrastructure to leverage relationships and grow the partnerships.

As you will read in the following stories, these business folks quickly recognized something of strategic importance. In most developing countries the majority population live on a dollar or so a day, conducting informal microenterprise, buying and selling for individual income needs. They typically employ the owner and perhaps a family member. This sector has traditionally been funded through NGOs. On the other end of the continuum is a very small percentage of highly successful large businesses that are able to access commercial banks for capital requirements.

Meanwhile, small and medium-sized businesses are virtually ignored and are often referred to as the "missing middle" of developing economies. These companies have managed to make the leap (and it is a big one) to the formal sector. They are legal entities that have employees, make payroll, and pay taxes. Their capital needs exceed the ceiling of the microlenders, but are too small for the commercial banks. Yet they are the business sector that has the potential to create the greatest number of sustainable jobs. They are also the high-impact entrepreneurs who can gain maximum benefit from a North American partner—someone who is willing to come alongside as a mentoring and financial partner, providing what Thomas Friedman, author of The World Is Flat, identified as Africa's greatest need: patient capital.

From that small beginning our Kenya partnerships have grown steadily over the past 10 years. The Christian Entrepreneurs Savings Society (CHESS) was formed in 1998 and now exceeds 400 members. Business leaders in Mombasa soon followed their lead and formed The Full Scale Business Group, which serves 200 businesses. Partners members also initiated a community water distribution cooperative that currently serves 10,000 people in the rural community of Kisayani; an amaranth production and distribution network that has helped transform the lives of over 500 growers in western Kenya; and Computers for Schools Kenya, whose training centers serve hundreds of schools that have equipped thousands of young Kenyans for jobs in the rapidly growing Internet sector of the economy.

Gitithia Rural Agro Finance, one of our newest affiliates in Kenya, started with 70 members and has grown to 2,500 small businesses with $1 million in loans. Since its inception, more than 2,000 jobs have been created and sustained. The executive secretary, Jennifer Githinji, calls herself "just a housewife." But she and so many of our other partners are not "just" anything. Like John Matheri, whose story you're about to read, they are amazingly competent, skilled, and dedicated business-people with a passion for serving others that frequently puts me to shame.

In Kenya the movement of "missioneurs," or missionary/entrepreneurs, is strong. Kenyans are leading the way in mentoring, coaching, and blessing their partners in-country, just as they have been blessed by their partners in North America. It's like fission: once the process of "people helping people help them-selves" has started, it's hard to stop it, especially when the primary impetus is the love of Jesus.

That love was, after all, the same motivation that caused a small group of New Testament disciples to be labeled "those who are turning the whole world upside down."

"There is a lot more to life than running your own company and becoming financially successful."

Milt Kuyers

Redefining Success

BY TIMOTHY STONER

O ver breakfast at the Hampton Inn in Vicksburg, Mississippi, one of the founding board members of Partners Worldwide, Milt Kuyers, is sharing with me a memory that determined the trajectory of his life.

It happened in his family's kitchen. Milt was 11 years old. His parents were talking, and several of the children, including Milt, were listening in. Their father said he had decided to ask for a bank loan because he believed God wanted him to give $1,000 to the capital fund drive of a local Christian school. At that time, he was a factory worker making $80 a week. Although Milt's parents understood and practiced faithful biblical stewardship, Milt's mother was taken aback by her husband's desire. Paying their bills was already difficult, and since the family had no savings, she knew that they were simply incapable of raising that money.

The next day Milt's father met with the bank manager. Milt recalls, "That evening, Dad came home and my mom asked him what the manager's response had been. He didn't say a word. He just dropped down on a kitchen chair, bowed his head, and began crying. Through his tears he

Milt never forgot the depth of his dad's emotion at being prevented from giving what he believed God wanted him to give.

told her that the bank had not granted him the loan because the officer did not believe they were able to pay it back."

Milt never forgot the depth of his dad's emotion at being prevented from giving what he believed God wanted him to give. As he tells me the story I can feel its impact on him, 60 years later. It has been imprinted on his mind and has served as an example and a motivation throughout his life. Today, after having started and sold six companies, and currently owning 12, Milt and his wife, Carol, live on less than 10% of their income. What his father was unable to give, Milt and Carol have given hundreds of times over.

Family Debt and Reconciliation

After graduating from the University of Michigan in 1958 with an MBA, Milt worked for seven years in private practice as a CPA for a large international accounting firm. He admits he was "on a single-minded mission to become highly successful." In pursuit of this goal he believed that he was ignoring his family and his relationship with God. He recognized that he needed to strengthen both areas.

As he was doing this soul-searching, an attorney from a leading law firm in Milwaukee called to ask if Milt would be interested in becoming the CFO of a manufacturing company that was poised to grow through acquisitions. Milt discovered that the CEO was a man who valued family, so he accepted the position along with its 40% pay cut. Four years later, at the age of 33, Milt was named president of the company's first acquired subsidiary.

Milt's dreams of financial success were being fulfilled, but a telephone call from his younger brother, Cal, derailed the trajectory of his comfortable life. It would put a halt to his plans for expansion and prosperity and would cause a wound that would take years to heal. The purpose of the call was to inform Milt that Cal was in serious financial trouble. The banks were getting ready to call in the loans on his businesses. He was facing bankruptcy. Milt agreed to go to Grand Rapids, Michigan, to talk things over.

At their face-to-face meeting Cal admitted that he had talked their father into guaranteeing his business loans. If his businesses folded it would take down their father, whose only asset was his home. Milt was furious but felt his only choice was to take responsibility for the notes.

The debt load took all of Milt's excess income and more. For several years he and his wife drove older cars. He recalls overhearing a conversation by a church member who clearly believed he had taken the infamous Dutch frugality to an extreme. Eyebrows were raised by those incapable of reconciling Milt and Carol's lifestyle choices with his position and salary as president of an apparently successful company. It comes as no surprise to hear him admit that he was extremely angry at his brother.

It took several years, but finally Milt was able to get Cal's debt paid off. During all that time there had been no contact between the two. Unaccountably, three days before his brother's 35th birthday Milt began finding it impossible to sleep. He was convicted about his deep resentment of his brother.

On the evening of his brother's birthday, Milt dialed Cal's number. He requested forgiveness for the anger that he had been harboring. As he spoke, Cal began to weep. He asked Milt's forgiveness for what he had done, and soon the two brothers were crying together. They forgave each other, and Milt's burden was lifted.

Three weeks later, Milt was at work when a phone call came. The message was that his brother had just died. Though deeply grieved, Milt was thankful that God had pushed him to reconcile with his brother three weeks before.

Heart on Fire

In 1984 Milt decided it was time to go out on his own. He began to look for a company he could purchase and turn around so that, as he puts it, he could "live happily ever after." While doing this, he was introduced to Star Sprinkler, a manufacturer of fire protection equipment that was on the ropes and needed new leadership. It was perfect for developing his skills in "turn-around" work.

Not long after, John DeHaan, a college friend and president of the Christian Reformed World Relief Committee (CRWRC), asked Milt to join eight other Christian Reformed businessmen at a MEDA (Mennonite Economic Development Association) conference in Charlottesville, Virginia. This Mennonite group was at the forefront of a movement to enlist businesspeople to get involved in building businesses and creating jobs in the developing world.

After the day's session, the nine men would go to John's hotel room and brainstorm how they could put the principles they had heard about into practice. Sometimes the discussions would extend almost to midnight. Their conversations centered on one question: how can businesspeople address the problem of poverty? Though focused internationally, they did not overlook the reality that there were serious local needs as well.

The late-night talks triggered something deep within Milt that was waiting to be awakened. He went back home with his heart on fire. He had been given an entirely new and ennobling vision of his role in the world. He now understood that he existed to do more than write checks for the church. For the first time he recognized that his position and skills as a businessperson were gifts from God, entrusted to him for a significant function in God's kingdom.

Milt now saw himself as a steward with unique, divinely bestowed abilities that were intended to have an impact beyond his family and even beyond his church. With that new awareness came a compelling sense of mission and a conviction that he was to begin in Milwaukee, where his business and his home were located. The task would be straightforward: providing work for the unemployed in the inner city.

Forming a Partnership Model

As he prepared his strategy and studied the challenges of poverty, Milt became convinced that the major problem for the poor was not finding jobs, but holding on to them. He concluded that it was essential to partner with an organization in the inner city that could provide the accountability to help unskilled workers develop the practices and habits needed to become valued employees.

Milt contacted several ministries in Milwaukee, but none had an interest in partnering with a businessperson. They were willing to receive his financial support, but they suspected his motives. He tried for six months, but the doors kept closing in his face.

Finally someone encouraged him to speak with Pastor James Carrington of Light House Gospel Chapel, a church in one of the most dangerous neighborhoods in the city. Before calling, Milt discovered that about 20% of the congregation was unemployed. He phoned Pastor Carrington and briefly explained his idea. The pastor agreed to meet and hear him out.

> He left with his heart on fire. He had been given an entirely new and ennobling vision of his role in the world.

A few days later Milt drove down to the church building at 35th and North to share his vision of partnering to provide jobs, accountability, and assistance so workers could succeed in their work. Pastor Carrington listened carefully. But when Milt was done he did not mince words. "I don't think it will work," he said. He was convinced Milt was a white employer on the lookout for cheap labor and good press. The pastor's experience had taught him that while white do-gooders might start strong, they usually failed to persevere when things became difficult. "The truth of it is," he explained, "I don't know whether I can trust you. If I went out on a limb with my people and then you decided to give up, I would lose significant credibility. I don't want to risk that you will give one member a job and then if it doesn't work out you'll just bail on the whole community."

Milt dragged himself back to his car feeling drained of his last hope. But at home he began to think the conversation over more calmly. A question struck him: Why did the pastor even agree to see me? Why invite me to come to his office just to tell me he didn't trust me?

Milt went to see Pastor Carrington a second time and repeated his idea almost verbatim. Again Pastor Carrington expressed his unwillingness to partner with Milt. He repeated his fears: "You will probably try this once and then when it gets hard you're gonna give up."

Milt left more discouraged than before. On his way back home he protested: "God, it was you who gave me this idea, but no one wants to help me bring it about. Why make me excited about something so wonderful if nobody is going to come alongside?" He again thought the conversation through. Something about it seemed almost staged, as if the rejection were somehow a test. He decided to call Pastor Carrington one more time. The afternoon of the meeting, as he was again winding his way through the narrow streets of Milwaukee's danger zone, Milt was battling anxiety mixed with the fear of being shot.

Once more Milt found himself sitting across the desk from the African American pastor. For a brief moment Pastor Carrington did not say a word. Then he leaned back in his swivel chair and said, "Mr. Kuyers, you are for real." It was a statement of fact laced with genuine surprise. Without pausing for any further discussion, the pastor told Milt that he could identify the unemployed members in his congregation who could make good, faithful employees. He told Milt he would call a meeting and invite them all to attend. But, he added, "I'm not sure how many will show up."

A few days later Milt and Pastor Carrington met with 19 people in the church auditorium. Pastor Carrington briefly introduced Milt and told them that this business owner had a great idea "and," he said, "I trust him." As Milt looked out at the group he saw hope in their eyes. What he did not tell them was that he had no idea what he was going to do with all of them. He had come to the meeting having identified only one job opening at Star Sprinkler.

Milt pressed forward and asked the group to write down their names, addresses, past work history, and job preferences. He thanked them, put the resumes in a folder, and drove home with them in his briefcase. Though he

A question struck him: Why did the pastor even agree to see me? Why invite me to come to his office just to tell me he didn't trust me?

had arrived at the chapel with a sense of excitement, he was leaving it in a panic. "What in the world am I going to do?" he groaned out loud. He had intended to hire one person, but now he'd created a sense of expectation for 19 people. What had seemed like an excellent idea just hours earlier appeared now to have been a huge error in judgment.

But in the next two weeks something unprecedented occurred. Orders came in so fast that Star Sprinkler needed to hire new workers immediately. All 19 members of Light House Gospel Chapel were put to work. Stable members of the church agreed to provide the accountability assistance needed to help their newly-employed members succeed. Transportation was offered for those who ran into difficulties getting to work. Light House began a daycare center to serve the single mothers who became part of the program.

Pastor Carrington remained personally involved. He made regular phone calls to Milt, alerting him when one of the church-member employees was having unusual difficulties. Through this partnership Milt and his friend James Carrington were able to impact more than 100 members of the Gospel Chapel.

As Milt finished his cup of coffee, he smiled at me. "That was the beginning of Milt the businessperson seeing there is a lot more to life than running your own company and becoming financially successful."

Hope, Purpose, and Transformation

A few years later John DeHaan called again, this time with an invitation for Milt to accompany him and some others on a "discovery trip" to Central America. Milt recognized that as executive director for the CRWRC, John might have a hidden agenda behind the call. "I knew that John was trying to build a stable donor base of businesspeople," he said, but he agreed to go anyway. The trip opened his eyes to the impact of Christian community development. The group was exposed to the dramatic contrast between a village with hope and purpose and one where the atmosphere is clouded with despair. Seeing with his own eyes profound economic, material, and spiritual transformation only deepened Milt's excitement.

> "That was the beginning of Milt the businessperson seeing there is a lot more to life than running your own company and becoming financially successful."

In 1992 Milt and Carol traveled with John and Alice DeHaan to Kenya on another "discovery trip." Also joining the group were Tony Betten, Marv and Joan Cooper, John and Margaret Vander Ploeg, Ed and Marcie Muller, Doris Tuinstra, and Meg Van Tol. Walking through the garbage dumps of Nairobi, which are home to hundreds of people, made a profound impression on them. They were used to seeing problems as challenges to be solved, but what they saw in the slum was overwhelming.

However, as they observed the substantial economic impacts in areas where CRWRC was making inroads, this oppression began to lift. They began to see the potential for businesspeople like themselves to make a significant contribution.

At each project the team would ask the development workers the same questions: "What happens when these microenterprises become successful? What is your strategy when they expand beyond meeting their immediate needs and begin hiring employees?" In each case the answer was the same: "There is none. They don't need us anymore. They are successful." The business owners were stunned. Not always as tactfully as they might have, they responded, "But, you *need* them!" They came to see that relief and development workers often looked at poverty through the lenses of social sciences rather than business. As a result, their focus tended to be on meeting the immediate basic needs (a good thing!), but not on broader economic sustainability.

These businesspeople understood immediately that successful businesses and businessleaders are essential engines to ending poverty. Not only will an expanding business create jobs, it can also help pay the bills that the agencies depended upon donations to cover. But as owners of companies and as hard-

Founding partners at Lanana House in Nairobi, 1997

headed realists, they also recognized that if a project cannot sustain itself there will come a day when the outside resources dry up and those who have been trained to be dependent will be worse off than before.

Milt and John Vander Ploeg decided to partner with John DeHaan in developing a funding arm for CRWRC comprised of businesspeople who wanted to do more than give money. Partners for Christian Development would be an organization that would measure success not by profit but by the number of jobs created. The vision was to link arms with capable entrepreneurs to help them succeed so they could in turn help their neighbors succeed. Ultimately, success would be achieved not when a family was able to feed itself, but when an entire community was freed from both poverty and charity.

It became obvious to Milt and to John Vander Ploeg that their first priority was to change the mindset of businesspeople. The revolutionary message needed to be delivered emphatically and unapologetically: business is not just business; in reality it is an outstanding Christian calling.

Business is not just business; in reality it is an outstanding Christian calling.

In 1997 Doug Seebeck took Milt and some of the other businesspeople back to Kenya to investigate a pilot project. They met with a group of successful businesspeople in Nairobi who had been gathering for weekly Bible study. The Kenyans described the unique cultural issues and needs of their country. Following these sessions there was an agreement that a real partnership as Christians for business development was possible.

The businesspeople broke up into two groups to hammer out the details. The North Americans sat under one shade tree in the Lanana House courtyard and the Kenyans under another. When they came back together they agreed to establish a $100,000 loan fund to be administered by an organization that would be called the Kenyan Investment Trust (KIT). It would be overseen by trustees from both sides of the partnership. The Kenyans committed to identifying trustworthy Christian entrepreneurs who needed loans to grow their businesses.

Looking back, Milt concedes that there might have been a strategic error in the formation of this first partnership. Despite its promising start, KIT was exclusively a loan organization, and the members were encouraged only to borrow, not save. That caused great difficulties, but it was an important lesson that resulted in a savings plan being hard-wired into all future agreements. It was implemented by Simon Ngeru in a new organization: CHESS (Christian Entrepreneurs Savings Society). It began with 25 businesspeople pooling their savings and has grown to include over 400.

James Gitao, a Kenyan trustee and KIT's chairperson, had a coffee farm that was facing financial difficulties. That same year James asked Milt if he would be interested in partnering directly together on his coffee farm. This called for a drastic re-evaluation of the role of the North American affiliate and its members. Prior to this time, the affiliate partnered by providing loans, advising, mentoring, and encouraging. There was no personal, individual financial risk involved. This invitation to become a viable partner "with skin in the game" caused no small consternation within the organization.

As Milt thought over the proposal, he explains to me, "It was obvious that there was no good, logical, or compelling reason to invest in the high-risk, culturally volatile, and business-unfriendly climate of Africa." But despite what his head told him, he felt convinced that the Lord still wanted him to do it. This was the first investment in what he would later call "heart entrepreneurship" or "leading with the heart." That heart investment has helped to save and sustain around 400 jobs in the coffee industry in Kenya.

More Than Playing Shuffleboard

Now in the latter decades of his life, Milt is a very content and fulfilled man. "At the age of 72 I have more joy than if I were spending six months in Florida playing shuffleboard and planning where to go next to eat out. I want to be doing something productive in God's kingdom." I sit up. He has gotten my complete attention. I am not used to this kind of language from a multimillionaire.

"There is no biblical precedent for self-indulgence," Milt continues. "That has nothing to do with God's kingdom. God nowhere encourages his people to 'eat and drink and take it easy now that you have reached your golden years.' In fact, Jesus spoke harshly about the wealthy businessperson who embraced that lifestyle. He warned that he will return when people least expect it and declare: 'This night your soul will be demanded since there is no place or purpose for you in my kingdom.'" This 72-year-old philanthropist takes a deep breath. He looks steadily at me and says, "I don't want to be one of the people Jesus has to speak to in that way."

Milt picks up his cup and finishes the last of the coffee. He shifts gears. "The strength that businesspeople bring to the table is that they have had a lot of experience with failure. They have learned to struggle and to overcome through dogged perseverance and a hard-won dependence on God. They understand that problems and obstacles are unavoidable. Success in only 1 out of 10 ventures is not grounds for discouragement; it is better than never having made the attempt. God makes it so hard. But, I've come to see that the struggles are God's way of saying: 'Milt Kuyers, do you know who is in control? You think you are so smart and that you can do all these things, but I'm the one who pulls the trigger. Although you have to keep pushing and struggling, I am going to open doors and close doors.'"

He smiles, but his eyes are very serious. "Through the adversity the successful businessperson has been taught the importance of not giving up. You still have to continue plowing forward through disappointments and discouragements. But if you have one success in the face of 10 failures, that's more than you would have had had you given up or not even made the attempt." Now he speaks more expansively as a member of the Partners board. "The businesspeople who are drawn to Partners Worldwide are folks who have learned through hard struggles to trust in God. These struggles have served to break them of their independence. Now they can joyfully celebrate what God has done, knowing that it was him, not them, that caused the success.

> # This 72-year-old philanthropist takes a deep breath. He looks steadily at me and says, "I don't want to be one of the people Jesus has to speak to in that way."

"The reality is that God needs moneymakers in his kingdom who will be faithful and responsible with the wealth he allows them to create. They are the ones who realize that stewardship is not really so much about what you give but what you allow yourself to keep." He continues describing the kind of stewards God is looking for. "Their goal is not to give a tithe and live comfortably on the rest, because they know that all their money is God's. They understand there is coming a day when they will have to give an account for what they justified to themselves they could live on."

I am stunned and convicted by the depth of this successful capitalist's commitment to a lifestyle I usually hear spoken of in the abstract. This son of a factory worker who could not give as much as he wanted is destined to hear the same words undoubtedly spoken to his own father: "Well done, good and faithful servant: enter into the joy prepared for you."

The beauty of it is that because of the wise choices Milt and Carol Kuyers are making now, they are experiencing that joy already.

Evelyn Hockstein

> "This partnership has greatly uplifted my business.
> Not only my business, but my mind."

John Matheri
Sewing School Pastor

BY TIMOTHY STONER

T he first thing John Matheri wants to be sure of is "that you are very okay with my ranguage, which is so row according to the standard of my education." Because John is from the Kikuyu tribe in Kenya, he pronounces the letter "l" as an "r."

We sit in a cement block structure with three small rooms. There are no diplomas or photographs on the wall, just a calendar and a few pictures torn out of a magazine. John's desk is small and battered. It's not anything like the typical North American CEO's office— but John isn't a typical CEO. He's a Kenyan entrepreneur and pastor, and he's also one of the humblest men I've ever met.

John's enterprise is a sewing school

This sewing school is, in reality, a very successful rescue mission that fronts as a trade school.

called Kihunguro Technical Training. It's located in rural Kenya in the town of Ruiru, one hour east of Nairobi. The school's name means "passing through." Most of those who pass through these doors are young women, but a few young men are learning trades here too. I will find out that this sewing school is, in reality, a very successful rescue mission that fronts as a trade school.

John continues in his broken English, which, though hard to follow at times, cannot disguise the depth of his commitment and compassion. "My background is so bad. You see me in this structure and it is so odd, to have unplastered walls and no cement floors. But for me, it is so smart." What he means is that this rustic, unpainted, and unvarnished grey building is an unimaginable improvement on the thatched hut he grew up in.

As we sit in his smart building, John begins to tell me his story.

From Drug Runner to Pastor

John's father was a truck driver. When John was about 5, his oldest sister began showing symptoms of mental illness. Another sister developed uncontrollable shaking of her right arm. John's family believed in a syncretistic Catholicism merged with African spiritism, so when doctors were incapable of determining the cause of either affliction, John's father hired a witch doctor to break the "curse." But it didn't work.

In order to support the family and pay the hospital bills, John's father began selling *muratina*, an illicit narcotic brew named for the trees whose seeds are ground, mixed with sugar and honey, and then allowed to ferment. Like the "white lightning" distilled in the hills of Appalachia, *muratina* is so powerful it can kill.

John's father also sold a narcotic called *banghi*. By the time John was 10, his father was using him as a "runner" to deliver the drug to customers. John says God protected him from using the drug himself, since the smell of the smoke gave him severe headaches.

In 1984, when John was 13, his father was apprehended and sent to prison for three years. John worked on the weekends herding cattle in order to pay for his school fees, uniform, and books, but he was only able to complete the 8th grade. Because his mother was unable to support the family, in 1990 he was sent to live with his uncle, who paid for John to learn the masonry trade.

While living with his uncle, John began to attend Christ Revelation Church. There he heard about Jesus and became a Christian. When she heard about his conversion, John's grandmother expelled him from the family compound because he was no longer a "Roman Catholic."

John helped his uncle build a second house, which became John's home. John began caring for his sister who was still troubled by severe shaking in her arm and shoulder. She was in constant pain—until the day John brought her to church, people prayed over her, and she was completely healed.

Some time later, John's faith moved him to start a local branch of the Compassionate Church. He began renting a small hall for 10 to 15 people. I ask him if he was the church's pastor. He shakes his head sheepishly and tells me, "No. I was just a small preacher." During my visit I find out that John Matheri's church has grown to 50 members who have recently built their own building, and John will be ordained the following Sunday.

The Entrepreneur Emerges

Then John begins to tell me the story of his business ventures. It's a roller-coaster ride of successes and setbacks.

In 1995 John married Margaret. The following year he built a small take-away food kiosk for her to run. She was in charge of the business and did all the cooking. Because John and Margaret couldn't afford tables and chairs, their customers sat on the ground to eat.

The kiosk did well, and John decided to branch out. He began a sewing business with Margaret's sewing machine and two employees. They made dresses, bed covers, and tablecloths. John brought the goods to various markets, some as far as 250 kilometers away, by catching rides on trucks that were traveling at night.

John's dream continued to grow. In 2002 a man named John Macharia, the bishop of Compassionate Church Pentecostal Fellowship, introduced John to CHESS—the Christian Entrepreneurs Savings Society. John obtained a loan of 70,000 shillings ($1,000) to expand the take-away food kiosk. He explains that it was impossible to qualify for a loan through the Kenyan banks because he had no collateral and the interest rate was high. In 2003 John received a second loan of 80,000 shillings ($1,200) for the purchase of two embroidery machines. The business grew to 10 workers using four machines, and John hired several young boys to take his products to market.

The troubles began when John's uncle and aunt died of AIDS. Because the food kiosk was on the uncle's land, the extended family, out of jealousy, demanded an exorbitant rent. The only option was for John and Margaret to abandon the business they had built together.

But John was not deterred. A year later he decided to construct a building for his tailor shop and training school. He borrowed 200,000 shillings (about $3,000) to buy land. John Vander Ploeg, Partners' North American Kenya Team Leader, who had met John Matheri during a visit in 2005, agreed to provide 486,000 shillings ($7,200) to pay for the cost of construction and installation of electrical wiring.

John stresses how grateful he is for the personal interest John Vander Ploeg took in him. Their partnership "has greatly uplifted my business. Not only my business, but my mind to have big vision." John admits that at first he had reservations about the mentoring, but when he saw John Vander Ploeg's genuine interest in him "my heart was filled with joy." John Vander Ploeg helped expand his perspective about what was possible for him as a business owner. He also made helpful suggestions for improvement. "I'm very greatly happy because of that," John says. "I think it could be very hard for me to have bought [this property] within this area, but through Partners it's uplifted me. So I really cry when I see what God has done through CHESS and through Partners."

But lately, circumstances beyond John's control have made things difficult again. Race riots broke out in early 2008 between supporters of the two main political parties that draw support from the two main tribes of Kenya (the Luos and the Kalenjin on one hand and the Kikuyu on the other), making it impossible for John's sales staff to get to their markets safely. The cost of living and materials increased greatly, and people's ability to purchase nonessential items such as tablecloths and bed covers dwindled. John has had to lay eight people off, but he allows them to bring in their own materials and use his machines free of charge so they can support themselves.

A Pastor in His Business

John gets up from his desk to show me around the school's three-room building. One room is being used to train young seamstresses. There are 12 girls, three of whom are doing beautiful and intricate embroidery work from memory. The designs have to be perfect; if they make a mistake the entire piece must be thrown away. Though they are very diligent and willing to learn, most of their families cannot afford to pay their school fees. After five months of training, John allows his students to bring in their own materials, make some products to sell, and pay back the school fees from the proceeds. Two of the girls are orphans; John is teaching them for free. Margaret reserves a spare bedroom in their home for girls who cannot afford to rent a place to live.

His answer is so gentle and humble it could melt stone.

I ask John if by training these girls he is concerned that they'll become his competition. His answer is so gentle and humble it could melt stone. "Brother, I have one thing inside my heart. I have a love toward youth. Because of my background and the challenges I went through, when I look at these young people they are hopeless and misused by everybody. We are in an area where people come in from many different tribes. There are 30 companies in our town, and we find that all these girls are being misused by men because of the poverty." His voice catches just a bit. "You can be totally . . ." John stops for a moment to gather himself. I find myself drawn to this unassuming man who carries within him God's broken heart for the wayward and the lost.

He goes on, "You can shed a tear when you come here late in the evening when you see the night clubs." He stops again as if weighing how to continue. He decides to lay it all out before me. "They pay only 100 shillings ($1.50) for the girls." There is such pain in his eyes and voice. It's like *he* can barely believe it.

I ask John where the desire to help these girls came from. He tells me that after he was born again he began to preach "the light of God." It comes out more like "right of God," and I figure this is not so far off. He says, "This is my area where I have been preaching. And giving the light of God without anything else, it cannot prevent a prostitute continuing in the prostitute life." What he is sharing is the practical reality James refers to in chapter 2:14-16:

> What good is it my brothers if a man claims to have faith but has no deeds? Can such faith save him? Suppose a brother or sister is without clothes and daily food. If one of you says to him, Go I wish you well; keep warm and well fed, but does nothing about his physical needs, what good is it?

In other words, it does little good to tell a prostitute about Jesus and then offer no alternative to help her break out of the snare of depravity driven by economic hopelessness. According to James, at least, that kind of faith is dead.

John's wife, Margaret, has done more than passively accept John's ministry; she has opened up her home to the young people. "Some of them, they are not yet transformed fully. We have been hosting them in our own house," John says. His family shares two rooms—one for their bedroom and kitchen, the other for their daughters—so that an extra bedroom could be made available "for our young ladies who cannot afford to rent a house."

We are sitting in his small office with a 15-year-old donated computer and stacks of papers. John looks toward the room where the girls are learning to sew, and his eyes light up. "Just last week," he recalls, his voice trembling with excitement, "our teacher here saw a student, one of the orphans, walking with a very notorious man, heading to his lodging." John called a counselor, found the girl, and brought her to the office. "We stayed in my office for more than three hours—she accepted Jesus, we prayed together, and now she is a born-again person." He is delighted.

> It does little good to tell a prostitute about Jesus and then offer no alternative to help her break out of the snare of depravity driven by economic hopelessness.

I ask John how many young people he has been able to rescue. He thinks for a moment and then answers, "About 200." Some have found employment and some have started their own businesses. John explains that his vision is to obtain funding so that he can afford to pay a counselor to come once per week to teach the girls. His goal is to educate them about the dangers of prostitution, *bhangi*, and drinking *muratina*.

It is clear that this is a businessman who is driven by something a lot bigger and more valuable than money. John is a pastor in his business before he is one in his church. He is pouring out his life and his energies to grow his tailor shop and training school so that lives will be rescued and transformed. He is doing much more than inviting people to church. He is taking Jesus with him into the marketplace and is saving hundreds of lives from economic despair and spiritual destruction.

Thanks to the mentoring help he has received from Partners Worldwide, John has a vision for the future as well. He tells me his dream for the second room: he wants to add building and construction courses as well as welding and carpentry so he can offer opportunities to more young men. "Rich people, they are using the young people in the clashes to fight other tribes. They are being incited to believe that our problems are because we have *that* president from *that* other tribe, and to fight. They are heading to any evil if only because they are given a few money." John's dream is to use his vocational school to free young men from callous manipulation and from self-destructive behaviors that are the poisoned fruits of endemic poverty.

Who's Teaching Whom?

It's obvious to me that running a training school isn't making John rich—it's actually losing him money—and his dreams for the future will only cost him more. But he wants me to understand something: "The purpose for having a technical school is not for me to make [a lot of] money. It is only to raise up our young people." He explains that if instead of using his machines to train young people he would hire workers to make bedcovers, he could sell the goods at a profit. "But I cannot close the school because then I will bring no change to the poor people."

> He is taking Jesus with him into the marketplace and is saving hundreds of lives from economic despair and spiritual destruction.

I ask, "What is the youngest girl you have trained and saved from prostitution?" He tells me and my heart wants to break. "She is not in this class," he responds. "It was last year. She was 13 years old." He struggles for words, finally saying, "It is paining."

For that 13-year-old's sake and for hundreds like her, I ask John if I can pray for him and his business before I leave. I am not able to steady my voice or keep the tears at bay as I pray. My prayer is that the Lord God, the Father of orphans, who sent his Son to bring good news to the poor, would have mercy upon my brother and prosper him and enable him to fulfill all the good desires of his heart.

I do not say it out loud, but my prayer is also that his brothers and sisters in North America would be freed from the distractions that capture their time, money, and energies to partner with this man who is quietly doing all he can to save the youth of his nation from an empty, wasted life and a cruel, degrading death.

As I stand up to leave, John again apologizes for his lack of education and his faltering English. I ask him please not to feel badly about it. It is I who am feeling the need to make an apology. This brother with minimal education and limited means is prompted by an obedient heart to use what little he has for the sake of others, and it is being multiplied a hundredfold. In North America, that is a rare story.

I leave the cement-block building, envious and motivated to greater obedience. Not for the first time I ask myself this question: In these international partnerships, who is teaching whom?

Kenya: Reflections   *by Doug Seebeck*

Our involvement in Kenya illustrates how important it is to keep learning from our experiences. What began with KIT as a good idea for developing entrepreneurs transitioned into a much healthier and effective model through the inclusion of a mandatory savings component. This was pioneered by CHESS under the leadership of Simon Ngeru. Each dollar saved would be matched by one dollar from the North American partners plus another dollar from the Partners Global Fund. In addition, five of the Kenyan members would guarantee the money being borrowed. This system has become so effective it is being replicated by partnerships in Kenya and in other countries.

The stories of Milt Kuyers and John Matheri also powerfully underline one of the core beliefs of Partners Worldwide: God is at work reconciling all things to himself through Christ, and God uses us as ambassadors of his reconciling love if we choose to follow him.

Reconciliation is a long-term process, however. God works in bits and pieces, sometimes more slowly than we like, but he does work. What God is doing through our partnerships in Kenya is a beautiful thing—not just through us, but in us.

Milt's story especially illustrates the disconnect that often occurs in Western culture: between faith and work, spiritual and secular, physical and spiritual, business and ministry, God on Sunday and work the rest of the week.

In numerous ways, Milt is fighting that mindset and, as he admits, is being changed as a result. In 1997 Simon Ngeru was visiting one of Milt's manufacturing plants in Milwaukee. As they were touring the facility Simon suddenly asked, "Milt, how many people do you employ in all your companies?" Milt did some mental calculations before telling Simon that he employed about 550 people. Simon shook his head in admiration and replied, "You have an awesome responsibility for 550 families, don't you?"

That observation changed Milt's business paradigm. He had always been a good employer who cared about his employees. But from that moment on, he resolved to care about their families as well. But Simon had also been impacted by the visit. When he returned to Kenya, he reorganized his tool and die operation and improved its productivity based on Milt's advice.

John Vander Ploeg's life was also enriched by choosing to partner with an inexperienced but compassionate entrepreneur. After a visit to Kenya in 2005, John Vander Ploeg told me about John Matheri. He said, "Doug, this is what it's all about. I know it's going to be hard for John to grow his business, because he has all kinds of obstacles against him, but I want to develop a personal mentoring relationship with him." And he did.

In 2008 when I visited Kenya, I knew I wanted to meet John Matheri. Martin Mutuku, our partnership manager, drove me to see the new facility John had been able to build. As I visited his employees and the young women who were learning a good and honorable trade, I felt my eyes welling up.

As I was leaving, John brought out a parcel. "Do you have room for a small package to take along when you return to the U.S.?" I nodded. He handed it to me and asked, "Will you please give this to John and Margaret in Kalamazoo?" I agreed. When I delivered the package, John Vander Ploeg opened it and showed me a beautiful handmade plaque. On it were these words: "And they grew in different worlds, walking in different paths, not knowing that one day they would come together as one." It was signed, "From your son, John." That gift was a symbol of the sweet fruit that is born from partnerships of brothers and sisters who share a love for business, a love for Christ, and a love for their neighbor.

When you're a follower of Jesus, the more you surrender, the more deeply you will be changed.

Through the lives of Milt and John I am convinced once again that there is nothing more powerful than people-to-people partnerships. When North American business partners return year after year to visit their international partners, using their vacation time and their personal resources, it speaks volumes of encouragement and integrity. And it's not just North Americans going off to faraway places—it just as often involves their international partners coming to shadow them in their businesses and to share their homes in the U.S. This impact is made possible as businesspeople choose to take seriously the challenge to follow Jesus in serving others.

When you're a follower of Jesus Christ, the more you surrender, the more deeply you will be changed. And the more you are transformed by God's powerful love, the greater is your desire to give your life away to serve others. As that happens, the journey becomes ever more exciting.

Nicaragua

The Context

BY DOUG SEEBECK

I n the fall of 1996, Gail and I attended our first parent-teacher conferences after being away from the States for 14 years. We had enrolled four of our five kids at Oakdale Christian School, an inner-city school in Grand Rapids, Michigan, that had the ethnic and economic diversity we were seeking. We didn't know many people and we were dealing with a bit of culture shock, so it was both comforting and surprising to run into Joel Huyser.

Joel was a member of Madison Square Church, our supporting and sending church in Grand Rapids and the place where Gail and I had met and married. I hadn't seen Joel and Jeannie Huyser in years, but while we were in Africa they sent us gifts and letters of encouragement as part of their work for the Madison Missions Committee. I was surprised to find out that Joel had recently decided to leave the practice of law and serve in Nicaragua with Christian Reformed World Missions (CRWM).

Joel pumped me for details about my new job. Since Partners Worldwide was only in the vision stage at that time, I gave Joel the most ideal picture possible of a new paradigm for mission. I sketched out our dream for connecting rich and poor in mutually transforming partnerships, for engaging business donors as full partners, and for an organization that would facilitate direct relationships among entrepreneurs instead of keeping them at arm's length.

Joel had been a business attorney for years, and he picked up on the concept immediately. He said, "That's something that could work really well in Nicaragua. I'll be in touch with you."

Joel was true to his word. We had several conversations, and 15 months later we sent a group of businesspeople to Nicaragua to begin exploring partnership opportunities with Joel and his team of local organizations.

Two years later, Darryl Mortensen, an international development veteran, walked into my office. He had been with the Christian Reformed World Relief Committee for nearly 30 years. He also was an old "aggie," having worked with Latino farmers in several countries, and he knew his stuff. He asked if I had a few minutes and proceeded to describe an exciting new pilot project he had worked on with CRWRC to utilize disaster funds.

Because CRWRC had significant undesignated money available following Hurricane Mitch in 1999, Darryl and his colleagues had been able to do something way outside the traditional community development box. It was a beautiful idea. They had bought a number of three-to-five-acre plots of land from *hacienda* (large ranch) owners who had no real interest in the properties but had a heart to help their countrymen. Darryl wanted to make those plots available to small farmers to help them get back on their feet.

Recognizing that this idea was outside CRWRC's core mission and that it would require large amounts of capital to purchase land, he wondered if Partners Worldwide could help.

I was thrilled with the idea. Granted, it doesn't take much to get me excited. My annual performance reviews have repeatedly listed the need to learn to say "no" as one of my main growth areas. But the truth of it was Darryl had a great idea and I *was* excited.

I recalled reading that, by some estimates, 85% of the rural poor in Nicaragua were landless. Most worked for absentee landlords, many of whom were living abroad, paying little attention to the land. It was frustrating to think that as we faced the beginning of a new millennium, thousands of farmers were still locked into what was essentially a feudal system.

"This is rather high-risk," Darryl explained. "It's a capital-intensive project that will probably require as much as $150,000 in order to get the attention of the *hacienda* owners." He was animated as he continued, "But this could be a strategy for a permanent solution to helping *campesinos* (small farmers) grow out of poverty."

Our board agreed to take the risk, but set some clear parameters. The idea was that we would start a Farmer to Farmer partnership. U.S. farmers would provide the capital; the local NGO would hold the title deed to the properties in the "land bank," be in charge of collections, and provide technical training for the farmers. We wanted there to be no confusion: the land would not be a donation. The farmers would buy it over a period of 7-10 years, and the U.S. partners would work with them on developing markets and business plans so that their farms would become agricultural enterprises, not just a source of food for subsistence.

The partners would commit to a minimum of one trip per year for encouragement and on-site evaluations, as well as to monthly phone calls for problem solving and mentoring. The repaid funds would be the basis for creating an in-country business development fund that would eventually be used to purchase new plots for more farmers. That is how Partners Worldwide began work in Nicaragua.

"We can make this whole community God's community."

Esteban Perez Dormuz

Landowner with a Dream

BY TIMOTHY STONER

Esteban Perez Dormuz's five-acre farm lies nestled on the slope of a mountain with a panoramic view that leaves you almost breathless. We are standing in front of his house, which is little more than a wooden shanty, but it's one with a million-dollar view. Several miles beneath us you can just make out a serene lake. Volcanoes (including some that look suspiciously active) spike up from the plains and valleys.

Esteban is a leathery, tough, but soft-spoken worker of the land. He's in his early 60s, and he carries himself with a dignity that is compelling. His son Juan Antonio, 33, stands quietly next to him. He does not say much, but it's not hard to tell that he loves his father and respects him deeply. There is an air of strength and leadership about Don Esteban. (In Spanish *don* means "sir" or "mister," and this man clearly deserves the Spanish honorific.)

Using his hands to emphasize the point he is making, Don Esteban says, "My father never owned anything. He even had to rent his own cot to sleep on at the large coffee plantation where he worked as a hired hand." Don Esteban is softening the painful truth. His father, and he himself, were little better than serfs. They served at the whim and plea-

They served at the whim and pleasure of the dueño, who paid them about 25 cents for an arduous 10-hour day.

sure of the *dueño* (the landowner), who paid them about 25 cents for an arduous 10-hour day.

Don Esteban's father worked six days a week, all year long, with no break. "He had very little time to be with his family, but he was the one who taught me to read," says Don Esteban. He has taken a seat next to me. He tells me that from his father he learned what to do, but also what *not* to do. "I never once saw my father intoxicated," he says, leaning forward in his chair. "He did not teach me any vices."

He leans back now to recount his early years before he became an owner of land. During the Sandinista revolt Don Esteban was one of the *acusados*, those unfortunate ones to be accused of being a communist. Many times the accusations were not true; often people's lives were threatened if they did not support the communists.

In the rugged mountains of north and central Nicaragua, most day laborers were assumed to be on the side of the "black and red"—the leftists. Since the Sandinistas were promising land to the landless, by definition all peasants had to be communists. It was an easy syllogism. But in Don Esteban's case, it was false. He was interrogated for three days, threatened with death if he joined the rebels, and released. Soon after, the Sandinistas forced him to "volunteer" as a freedom fighter. Opting to submit to one more master rather than die, he tied on the scarf and became a "communist." During a mortar attack on his station, he was wounded. Since he was no longer able to fight, he was released.

After Daniel Ortega defeated the Somoza dictatorship in 1979 and took power in the name of the people, Don Esteban did not get his own property as he had been promised. Desperate to grow his own food, he began farming on rented land while also teaching primary school and working on coffee farms. In early 2000 coffee markets took a dive and the massive coffee plantations began to fold, leaving thousands of laborers without work. Don Esteban's children worked side by side with their father on their rented land, but the family was barely able to live.

Don Esteban has been looking down at his hands as he remembers those difficult years. Then he lifts his eyes and nods his head. Smiling gravely, he continues, "God gave me a dream that I would one day work on my very own land and I would have strangers from another country visit me on that farm." He was convinced this dream had come from God and that it would, in fact, come to pass. He was right.

In 2005 Don Esteban heard about a land-bank named El Progreso. He applied for a plot of land, and in 2006 received a loan for $1,500 that enabled him to buy the acreage he now farms. Don Esteban is smiling. Taking just the barest pause for effect, he says, "And then, one day, farmers from Iowa came."

His smile exudes a quiet confidence. In his dream, God had shown him that these visitors would be part of God's plan to bless him. So he wasn't taken aback when tall gringos stepped onto his property for the first time to see how the crops were doing. The Americans were impressed. Every inch of ground was being used to grow food for consumption and high-value cash crops sought after by local and North American markets.

Don Esteban gets up from his chair and goes into his humble wooden house. When he returns, in his strong hands he gently cradles a framed picture. He proudly points to his family surrounded by a team of farmers. "The farmers from Iowa have mentored, encouraged, and prayed for me. Because of them I am now ready to help other landless farmers. I will tell them that they can do it. I can help them organize, and they can learn from my farm. And then we can make this whole community God's community."

The community Don Esteban is talking about numbers around 100,000, and 80% of them are landless day laborers. Don Esteban has a dream that is bigger than getting his own piece of the pie (or the mountain, in this case). He is not content simply to increase his yields and turn a good profit on his cash crops. He wants to see the lives of those who are still hopeless changed.

In 2006 Don Esteban's son Juan Antonio bought his own five-acre plot next to his father's. They work side by side as if their two plots are one farm. On those ten acres, their diversified crops include bananas, chayote (a pear-like vegetable), sugar cane, pineapple, a variety of other local vegetables including *frijoles* (red beans eaten three times a day whether you want them or not).

> # Don Esteban has a dream that is bigger than getting his own piece of the pie (or the mountain, in this case).

Much of their labor involves organically revitalizing the hard soil that has been overgrazed and eroded. Here mentoring has also helped. Don Esteban shows us the *lombreria* ("worm farm") that is being used to create compost. He would also like to build a pond to raise delicious tilapia fish.

He and his son are looking ahead. They both are current on their loans and expect to pay them off well before the 10-year term is up. Their 500 coffee plants should begin to produce soon, and they are nurturing 800 more coffee seedlings. They've planted more than 100 hardwood trees that will be harvested when Juan Antonio is 52. A good straight cedar, depending on its height, can go for $500; if it's cut into usable lumber, it may bring five to ten times that much. In a way, these trees are the son's retirement policy. Don Esteban, for the first time in his life, is able to look beyond mere survival and is making plans for the future of his son and his grandchildren.

"When I heard about the opportunity to move off the *hacienda* through the land-bank loan, I knew that my dream had come true." The elder farmer is smiling again. "The chance to actually own my own land was something I never could have imagined!"

We are looking out at the beautiful mountain view. It is quiet for several moments. Then Don Esteban looks straight into my eyes as he says, "My life has totally changed. I have been called by God to do this, and I am going to work

"My life has totally changed. I have been called by God to do this, and I am going to work in his garden until the day I die."

in his garden until the day I die, to bring God glory forever!" Goosebumps race up my arms. Less than two years ago this man had nothing. He had no hope and no vision. Now he is talking with a humble certainty and a quiet boldness about being a vessel to help transform an entire community of desperately poor people in the name of Jesus.

Speaking in purely pragmatic terms, this transformation only cost about $1,500, plus some mentoring by the local Nicaraguan promoter (financed in part by Partners Worldwide) and yearly visits by North American farmers Don and Bonnie Vos. By any business standard that would be considered seed money with a monster yield. In reality, it is kingdom economics on display: a willing person, a few "loaves and fish," and suddenly thousands are fed.

What gives Don Esteban as much joy as watching his "garden" flourish is seeing dreams restored. He loves to be a part of giving hope "to those whose visions for the future have been squelched, whose minds and hearts have been shut down." He is surrounded by people like himself who have great ability and dedication but no expectation for their future. That's a reality he hopes to change.

He says, with his eyes sparkling, "I poured out my youth on land owned by wealthy landowners. Now in my old age I have found hope. I want others who are like I was to get their own land, and I want to bring them ideas and encouragement. I want to help others who have little or no vision to find hope."

At that point I put down my notepad. I figure that Don Esteban has said about all that needs saying.

"We are learning to pray crossculturally."

Don and Bonnie Vos

Farmer to Farmer

BY TIMOTHY STONER

My wife, Patty, and I are trekking up and down very steep mountains in Nicaragua with Iowa farmers Don and Bonnie Vos. They co-lead the Farmer to Farmer affiliate team here, and we're tagging along as the team sets out to visit land-bank members to see how their farms are doing.

As we travel, we tell our stories. Patty and I learn that the Vos family farm is located in Oskaloosa, halfway between Des Moines and Iowa City. Don and Bonnie started their life together with nothing. Neither had the jump-start provided by growing up in the home of a cattle, corn, or pig baron. On their wedding day they hadn't received 1,000 acres as "a little something" to get them going. What they had was one pig.

Don and Bonnie worked to exhaustion to grow their farm. Now, 36 years later, they have a total of 2,000 acres they either own or rent on which they raise 8,000 pigs and 200 head of cattle. So when they encourage the Nicaraguan farmers we're going to visit, they speak directly out of their own life experience.

I watch as Don carefully asks the Nicaraguan partners about the disease that is attacking their *frijoles*. These beans are, arguably, the most essential consumption crop in the country. If the

> On their wedding day they hadn't received 1,000 acres as "a little something" to get them going. What they had was one pig.

frijoles don't grow, the impact on the Nicaraguans is the same as if a virus suddenly made all the hamburgers in the United States inedible. It's really worse than that, since in Nicaragua *frijoles* are usually found on the dining table at every meal, including breakfast.

Don has been researching the bean disease with his son, Jason, whom I tagged "Tex." (What else could I possibly call a young man who stands 6'7," weighs barely 195 pounds, and gets off the plane in Managua wearing blue cowboy boots, a white cowboy hat, a bandana, and boot-cut jeans with a tin of "chaw" in the back pocket?) Tex's dad later lets me know that his son's involvement with the mountain farmers is just one of the unexpected blessings that have come from partnering with the Nicaraguans.

Don shows several farmers some Internet research that lays out a battle plan for combating "red rust," which he is pretty sure is the culprit here. There is a relatively inexpensive organic pesticide the farmers can make to defeat this dastardly microscopic foe. He encourages them to discuss it with Miguel Angel, the local land-bank director.

The farmers who have not yet moved onto their land are strongly encouraged to do so soon, since productivity increases dramatically when the farmer lives on his property. It can save an hour or more of transportation time, avoids wasting precious *cordobas* on a rental shack, and allows the farmer to better protect his crops, since theft is a major problem. Don asks about their plans for diversification and their long-term strategy. He takes a look at their crops and their worm farms. He spends more time encouraging the farmers than offering advice.

> He takes a look at their crops and their worm farms. He spends more time encouraging the farmers than offering advice.

Inevitably, and he will do this at each farm, he also will ask how they are doing in their relationship with Christ. This is not an incidental matter. While growing the farm is of great importance, it is not more important than the farmers' relationship with God. The Iowa farmers know well that it does not matter if you gain thousands of acres of tillable, fertile soil but lose your own soul in the bargain.

So Don prays for each farmer at the end of the visit. He prays for continued blessing on their land, good health, and good weather. He also prays that they would continue trusting in Jesus and get to know him better all the time. This Iowa farmer has become a sort of priest, and it is a beautiful and holy thing to see.

From Iowa to Nicaragua

Wendy Van Klinken, Farmer to Farmer co-partnership manager along with her husband, David, drives us back to our hotel in La Dalia, about 45 minutes from the farms. The town is mostly one long street that splits into two streets lined with crowded little shops. We walk six steps down from the pavement where we have parked the Toyota HiLux. The entrance of our hotel is marked by a nondescript green metal door set into a wall that says "Hotel America" in large letters. Something tells me that this hotel might be catering to the ubiquitous relief-worker clientele.

Inside, each room has a ceiling fan that works, a TV that sort of works, and a shower that offers cool to cold water. I have been in places where the showers came from black solar bags, so I am very okay with the amenities.

> "Once we met the farmers in Nicaragua, we loved it. We became connected right away. Now we can't turn back anymore."

Before we arrive, Don Vos tells me how he came to be in a small town in Central America, 2,225 miles as the crow flies from his farm in Oskaloosa, Iowa. He speaks straightforwardly, like you'd expect. "We saw an announcement in a bulletin from our church that said a group was going to Nicaragua to work with farmers, so we thought it would be something we'd really like doing." The year was 2001.

"Once we met the farmers in Nicaragua, we loved it. We became connected right away. So when the time came to return the next year, we decided to go back again. Now we can't turn back anymore. We just have to go back to see them. We've become friends, we know them by name now, and we have a very good time when we come to visit."

Don has left a lot out. I was curious about the difficulty of adjusting from life on the Iowa farm to the daily struggle for survival on the Nicaraguan mountain slopes. As I suspected, it was not easy for the North Americans. "Well, the first year was culture shock, really. We didn't understand the culture. We didn't understand the farming practices and we couldn't imagine their living conditions." Being farmers rather than typical North American tourists, they ate the same food the Nicaraguans did. "It was basically rice three times a day." He has run out of words to describe the clash. "It was culture shock," he repeats. "But after the second year we could begin to understand what some of their struggles were and what they have to battle to get things to grow successfully in Central America."

Don is a humble man. He did not come here full of Western agrarian wisdom to impart to "the poor Nicaraguans." He has learned to be quick to hear and slow to speak. It was not until he and Bonnie had come to visit their land-bank owner friends for the third and fourth time that they were able "to begin to give just a bit of advice." Since they've visited consistently for seven years now, the Nicaraguans often look to the Iowa farmers to answer questions, but, Don says, "Before, it wasn't like that. We were just visitors before we developed a personal relationship with them."

Dignity First

Like all wise people who come to serve Christ among people in the developing world, Don and Bonnie had to learn to suppress the natural tendency to meet every need through charity. "That's the first thing we wanted to do. The first reaction was to say, 'We have access to so many things, let's go to the store and bring it back for you.'" It's the logical reaction of the compassionate heart.

But Don and Bonnie learned that in a culture of poverty, handing out gifts only encourages passivity. Of course, where disasters of one sort or another have brought utter devastation, gifts of compassion are essential. However, this is a temporary, transitional context. Relief must become restoration that results in liberation. The sooner this occurs, the better for everybody.

What the landowners prize is the knowledge that they are not laboring alone.

Continual handouts rob the poor of something precious: the human need for self-respect and dignity. It communicates to the poor that they are incapable of ever becoming productive, fruitful image-bearers of God. Charity, while building up the giver, erodes and undermines the recipient. With one hand it gives and with the other it takes away.

The Nicaraguan farmers' lives bear this out. They do not look forward to the Iowans' visits so they can get goodies. They are not dependent upon these wealthy North Americans to provide what they need. They have the quiet confidence of people who have hope and pride. Their hands are not held out to receive, but to give back.

On more than one occasion I am told that what the landowners prize is the knowledge that they are not laboring alone. They are in a struggle, but it is one that is also borne by others who understand and who have succeeded. Their faces tell the story. They are just so happy to see their friends coming back and to have another chance to show off the good work they are doing.

Praying Crossculturally

Don is not given to self-promotion. He is uncomfortable when the spotlight is turned his way and would rather keep to the background. But I press him for a response from a farmer that has been particularly gratifying, and one does come to mind. "Well, in the last few days, more than one of the farmers have said that our visits have given them hope and have inspired them to continue to work and to continue in their faith in Christ."

Don and Bonnie know the farmers by name. Don recalls an example that illustrates their close relationship. "Several years ago, one of Calixto and Ramona's sons was murdered. We mourned with them and prayed for them. And when we came we grieved with them." He repeats it as if I would have trouble believing it. "That's really what happened." He continues, "This year when we came, the family was happy, and I like to think we helped them. But they taught us, too. They didn't lose faith. They hung right in there. It goes both ways. We have learned from them and they from us."

He is convinced that these personal connections are what makes the Farmer to Farmer program so successful. This is not a traditional North American missions trip where you do a project, build something for an anonymous poor person, then leave, never to return. "It's not a one-time visit; it's a continual going back. They know us; we know them and their struggles. Through the year we remember and pray for them. They're like our own families. We have pictures of them. They have pictures of us, so we can send emails and they can pray for us too."

Bonnie, who has been listening in, adds, "Those emails are filled with questions like, 'How is so and so? How can we pray for you?' We're starting to see this reciprocal interest, and it almost makes us cry. Because this is *huge*. To have them send letters to another country they know nothing about to people they barely know is just amazing."

Establishing close relationships with farmers in the mountains of Central America has changed Don and Bonnie's lives. Their values and priorities are not the same: "It isn't about getting 'things' so much now, but about serving others." The trips to Central America can be demanding, physically and financially. But they still look forward to them. "We just love coming. Our daughter moved out here for a year and worked with Dave and Wendy Van Klinken, and now our youngest son ("Tex") is here on his second trip. He says he won't skip it. He wants to keep coming. He's had some tough times in his life . . . but he's coming around."

The expression on Don's face is one of deep contentment. The Vos family has navigated troubling waters, but serving farmers in Nicaragua has had an

Don and Bonnie Vos (right), their son Jason, Sarah Vander Hart (back left), and the Miguel Reyes family of the El Congo land bank

David Van Klinken

unforeseen benefit. It has somehow changed his son's life. "All of this is a part of him coming around and acknowledging that Jesus is a part of his life too."

Don stops for a moment. I wasn't expecting it, but this strong, lean farmer from Iowa is tearing up. I am too. "God is faithful!" Don declares. "He is always faithful to us and to all these people." It is a farmer's doxology: "Rain . . . sunshine. We don't always get it like we'd like, but God is faithful! The Nicaraguans experience it just like we do. They are dependent on it even more than we are. We have electricity, air conditioning, motor vehicles, and so much more, but everything they do is by the sweat of their brow."

I am glad that Don does not seem to be embarrassed. I know he comes from a tradition that isn't always comfortable with showing emotion. He then adds something that is very large and missiologically rich, but to him it's just the truth as he sees it about their new reality: "We are learning to pray crossculturally."

It Comes Down to Love

I am surprised to hear of the response Don and Bonnie have received from some church members. Perhaps I should not be. "They really don't understand why we would take 10 days of our time and our own money to come over here so we can sleep on a cot or on the floor and go up and down roads we can't even dream of. They think we're basically out of our minds."

This pains him, I can tell. Not only is the trip physically and financially demanding, there is also a spiritual cost on the return. It is hard to share your joy with those who look at a trip to visit farmer friends living in shanties on the slopes of Matagalpa as an irrational foray into the absurd.

I ask, "What might bring a change in perception?" Don does not really have to think all that hard—perhaps he has mulled this over before. "I think the Spirit of God has to bring it home to people that we are not number one. Self is not number one. You have to come to that. That's the only way it will happen."

> "The Spirit of God has to bring it home to people that we are not number one. Self is not number one."

He then refers to the community-wide celebration we had just participated in: all the land-bank owners and their families gathering together to give the team its thanks. They sang, danced, and played music for us. They also laughed as the North Americans made fools of themselves in a humorous skit my dear wife thought up. Throughout the community party the gratitude from the new landowners was palpable. It was a touching and memorable occasion.

"To see them, how they come out on an afternoon like we've just experienced. Just to think how we met together, played together, prayed together today. I can't think of a better way to worship than what we did this afternoon. Any church service you could try to arrange couldn't beat it." Don's eyes are filling up again. "I get emotional over it."

He is having a hard time getting the words out. Although generally stoic by nature, this lanky farmer from the heartland of North America is now crying. The depth of the appreciation he has just witnessed and the joy of participating with these farmers living in the mountains of Nicaragua has gripped him.

Don tells me that he wouldn't trade the delight of partnering with these farmers for months lounging in the Caribbean or in Mexico or on any other luxury vacation he can imagine. Those things don't hold a candle to the joy he and his family experience walking up and down seemingly impossible slopes. Words escape him. He shakes his head. "There is so much more to life than indulging yourself."

On the drive back to Managua, David Van Klinken explains that "it all looks good on paper when you are laying out plans for a program. The original idea was that mentoring was going to be the key. But what we found out was different. The foundation of Farmer to Farmer is a Christian brotherhood and sisterhood."

He illustrates this by relating a story he overheard a few hours earlier. After a visit to the last land-bank farm, Don Vos gave the farmer a Latin embrace (the Iowans have learned to loosen up). For some reason, before leaving Don asked, "What else do you want from us? What would you like?" It is not the usual question. It is actually one that the Iowans, early on, learned to stop asking. David, who has been expertly dodging potholes as he drives, looks at me briefly. He tells me that the Nicaraguan farmer looked up at the lanky Iowan who owns 400 times more acreage than he does and said, "Just please come back."

The relationship these two farmers have forged is not about money or knowledge. It comes down to love: the rich and the poor entering each other's lives so that the love of Jesus can bring transformation of the heart—on both sides. Material, logistic, and economic changes will come in due time. For Don and Bonnie Vos and their Nicaraguan partners, that's what it's all about.

"Their aim is nothing less than a nation of businesspeople on their knees before God."

Roberto and Rosa Espinoza

Business in the Barrio

BY TIMOTHY STONER

R oberto and Rosa Espinoza, a dynamic young Nicaraguan couple, are telling me their story. Like all of the stories I've collected on this trip, theirs is an amazing account of what happens when business and mission go hand in hand.

Strangely enough, Roberto and Rosa met in the Ukraine in 1989, where they were studying at the Politechnic University of Odessa. Although they were not communists, they had both received a highly coveted scholarship from the Sandinista government of Daniel Ortega. They modestly claim that receiving these awards was a matter of the grace and favor of God, but their superior grade point averages must have helped too.

The two fell in love, married, and graduated in 1994—he with a degree in electrical engineering and she in economics. They returned home to Nicaragua with a child in tow, never dreaming what God had in store for them.

Hands and Feet

After the Espinozas returned to their country, their pastor, Ricardo Hernandez, began teaching the congregation about the importance of biblical business principles. He also presented them with a direct challenge: "You are the hands and feet of Christ. Don't just pray that God will help the needy—maybe you're the answer to your own prayers." The pastor's point was simple, strong, and clear: you can be a good Christian *and* be a good businessperson.

These messages stirred Roberto, somewhat to his consternation. At the time, he had a good position with World Vision as the Director of Special Projects/Disaster Relief. There was no reason for him to leave a comfortable position with its fringe

"You are the hands and feet of Christ. Don't just pray that God will help the needy—maybe you're the answer to your own prayers."

benefits and its respectability. After all, he had his wife and now six children to think about. But his pastor's exhortations continued to disturb him.

He finally gave in. Despite having absolutely no business experience, he decided to take the pastor's challenge to heart and start a business from scratch. After planning methodically in excruciating detail, as only an engineer can, Roberto launched Royal Wood in 2005. It would manufacture high-end doors made from cedar, mahogany, and other precious woods. Rosa decided to start a butcher shop.

They gathered a group of 27 Christian business owners who would meet together for mutual encouragement and support. They also agreed to pool some money to set up a loan fund to help others begin their own businesses. They initially called themselves *Negocios Cristianos de Nicaragua* (NCN), but later changed their name to *Red de Profesionales de Nicaragua* (Network of Nicaraguan Professionals) because of their desire to have a broader impact in the larger business community. With the organization's loan fund, they helped start 22 additional businesses.

Encouragement in Action

As it happened, Pastor Hernandez had a boarder living in his home: a young American named Bob Vryhof, who had been hired by Partners Worldwide in 2004 after graduating from Calvin College with a degree in business administration. Bob recalls that Pastor Hernandez's messages "were very convicting."

When Bob heard about Roberto and Rosa's network, he helped them forge a connection with Partners Worldwide in 2006. A year later a revolving loan fund of $80,000 was provided to be distributed among owners of small- to medium-sized businesses. Roberto would oversee the fund as the project manager, assisted by Rosa. That year, the fund provided loans to eight businesses. Partners Worldwide also agreed to help provide instructional materials to assist the network with business planning, finances, development, and ethics using biblical principles. In 2008 there were around 60 members in the network.

Roberto's role was to administer the funds, provide and organize the training, and monitor the business owners to encourage their success and faithful loan repayment. Rosa would screen the 12-page business plans and evaluate the information provided. Loans would not be provided to start-ups, but to business owners who had a desire to expand their existing enterprises. The goal was to create jobs in Nicaragua, where unemployment rates were overwhelming. Whereas the going commercial interest rate was between 30% and 40%, and the standard for NGOs was around 25%, Partners Worldwide agreed to charge only 9% to cover the costs of the program.

Growth was slow. There was a need for much more than capital. Most of the business owners had no vision for the future. The crushing obstacles to business growth they faced daily had narrowed their vision to one thing: survival.

Roberto and Rosa's task became that of breathing life back into men and women with the barest pulse of hope. They encouraged struggling entrepreneurs to ask themselves, "Where does God want to take me? What is his desire for me? What has he put on my heart?" Today, scores of Nicaraguan businesspeople have been freed to dream and to begin using their gifts and talents to the maximum.

One of the areas where Roberto and Rosa's encouragement has been most helpful is in promoting effective time management. In a culture of *mañana* that values relationships much more highly than schedules, studying strategic use of time is almost unheard of. Nevertheless, simple innovations to maximize efficiency have proved revolutionary.

Where once these businesspeople believed that not-failing was success, their vision has been raised to see that they are blessed men and women, empowered not to simply receive blessings but to be a blessing to their families, their communities, and their nation. Employees are no longer viewed as workers to be exploited for personal profit, but as people created in God's image to be cared for, valued, and treated with dignity and respect.

> Roberto and Rosa's task became that of breathing life back into men and women with the barest pulse of hope.

Business to Business (or B2B, as it is better known), the partnership between the North Americans and the Network of Nicaraguan Professionals, is helping 18 small to medium businesses that include a butcher shop, an auto parts store, a hammock manufacturer, a carpenter, a woodworker, and a belt-maker. Two shops specialize in making *guayaberas*—traditional elaborately hand-decorated shirts worn by government officials. Many of these enterprises had struggled under microloans with other institutions at interest rates of 30% percent or higher. When these businesses receive a loan from Partners Worldwide, they use part of it to pay off these usurious debts.

Business in the Barrio

Roberto and Rosa have themselves been empowered in this process. They beam when speaking of the level of confidence that the North Americans have placed in them, and the joy of having their own gifts affirmed. "They have entrusted us with so much. Over and over they continue to show us how much they trust us." He flashes me a grin. "Nothing—nothing is more important than relationships!"

While the financial and technical help they receive from Partners Worldwide has been incalculably important, Roberto emphasizes that it is the relationships

"Nothing— nothing is more important than relationships!"

with North American businesspeople based on respect and transparency that has had the most profound and lasting impact. Though he and Rosa are successful task-oriented business owners, administrators, and business mentors in their own right, their conclusion is unanimous: "Relationships are everything." And, they add with a bit of humor, "Strategic relationships are even better."

Their own gifts and callings have been so affirmed that they are leading their network in sacrificial servanthood. Every Thursday from 9:00 to 11:00 a.m. they make the drive to the most despicable, degrading place in the capital city. Every major city in Nicaragua has one: a community that has grown up on top of and around the main garbage dump. In Managua this community is called *La Chureca*. The name is virtually a curse word. It refers to something that is twisted, blighted, and broken. Roberto and Rosa refuse to use the term. They call it, instead, *El Barrio*: "The Community."

Their calling is to do more than give gifts or speak nice, easy words. Many NGOs and church groups visit the dump on sporadic missions of mercy but do not share the Espinozas' vision for the long-term physical benefit of the 800 people who live there. Most see the poverty and come with temporary assistance that is used up immediately, only to leave behind an intolerable emptiness along with an insatiable, gnawing need. What the people in the community need is not only food for today but hope for tomorrow. This is what Roberto and Rosa are intent on providing.

Their message is simple: "Jesus loves you. He says that you are valuable and have a purpose on this earth. He promises that your life can have meaning." They tie these words to practical information about developing good work habits and a successful business. At the beginning, Roberto asked the people to write down their vision for the future, but he learned they didn't know how to write. So he asked them to draw a picture of their future dreams instead. For most, it was just getting out of the hellhole they called home.

He asked them to draw a picture of their future dreams. For most, it was just getting out of the hellhole they called home.

Roberto and Rosa are on a scouting mission. They come to the dump seeking out desperate people who, despite having nothing, yearn to provide for the needs of their families and ultimately break the stranglehold of their toxic environment. Every day, the dump-dwellers face the smells of putrefying waste and decomposing garbage, swarms of flies and plague-carrying mosquitoes, and filthy water. Always and everywhere there is stinging, burning smoke from fires that burn perpetually. It is a miracle that only some of the children struggle with a persistent and debilitating cough. On the day that my wife and I accompanied Roberto and Rosa in their red Suzuki APV van, moving through the polluted air was like trying to find your way through a blizzard in Michigan. But *this* snowstorm smelled like sulphur, burning and grabbing at the back of your throat, threatening an irrational claustrophia.

Thus far, Roberto and Rosa have found 26 individuals willing to admit to a seemingly absurd desire to create a business in *El Barrio*, whether recycling plastic, paper, metal, and glass, or raising pigs. A few have accepted the challenge of starting small *pulperias*—tiny shops that stock items ranging from soap, soda, and bottled water to combs, canned food, and candy. Since these start-ups are too small to qualify for B2B loans, Roberto and Rosa have been making personal loans to help two of these storefronts get off the ground. Every week they meet with the owners and others interested in starting some business venture among the community of 800 shrouded in smoke. They help write up business plans and provide the opportunity for business training at a level that even the most established business owners in Managua have never had access to.

But, while focusing on economic issues, they know that the people who live in the dump have spiritual needs too. If Jesus visited *El Barrio* he might say, "What does it matter if the poor succeed in business so that they are able to stuff merchandise from the whole world into their stores, but wind up losing their souls?" This Nicaraguan couple concludes that, according to the Lord of rich and poor, employment is an important goal, but it is not the most important one. They are convinced that what the poor need most is Jesus.

So on Saturdays they return to the dump with a young couple commissioned to start a new church there. They come to join with 30 or so squatters to worship the Christ of the poor, the Christ who came proclaiming good news for all. They raise their voices to the One who promises them freedom—freedom from bondage to sin and its curse and from poverty's horrible vortex of despair, despondency, and empty, meaningless existence.

Future Goals

Since Roberto and Rosa joined with Partners Worldwide four years ago, 120 new jobs have been created and 60 existing jobs have been preserved. In an environment of pandemic unemployment, this is a miracle and cause for celebration. Due to the Espinozas' positive leadership and keen ability to detect potential in the candidates applying for loans, every one of the 18 loans they administer are current.

Working with Partners Worldwide has opened doors to other relationships. One of the most unexpected is the Espinozas' connection with the prestigious MBA program of Wake Forest's Babcock Graduate School of Management. Through an encounter with Christopher Yuko, a grad student who was doing research in Managua, a pilot program has been created where graduate students at the University's School of Business get hands-on experience with real businesspeople needing real-world business mentoring help in one of the poorest countries in the Americas.

After graduating in 2007, Christopher moved to Managua to set up the extension program for Wake Forest. That means that at least twice per year these Nicaraguan entrepreneurs, some of them illiterate, several of them living on top of a fetid dump, are receiving business training from some of the best and brightest in North America.

Roberto and Rosa point to this as a classic example of strategic relationships. Through Partners Worldwide, what would have been unthinkable has happened: those who were once unemployed, without a hope in the world, living in the most degrading conditions possible, are being taught how to succeed in business by some of the most privileged business minds in the world. And so the dream is being fulfilled: the rich and the poor are being brought together to help eradicate poverty.

"Their aim is nothing less than a nation of businesspeople on their knees before God."

I ask Roberto jokingly if he has any long-term goals. He looks at me to see if I am pulling his leg. Of course he has goals—he is an engineer and a master business mentor. "In four years I want to start a credit union," he informs me. "With how much?" I ask. He is aiming for an initial capitalization of 500,000. For a minute I am thinking in dollars. "Cordobas," he explains. That makes it approximately $26,000. "And I want us to provide 100 new jobs."

But this talented Nicaraguan couple has not forgotten what is of highest importance. They refuse to only look at the material needs and the physical problems of those they serve. While envisioning the creation of scores of new businesses and 100 more jobs, they also want to see a healthy church started in *El Barrio*. Roberto confides in me that he has also been feeling God calling him to start a church in their own neighborhood. "He has always wanted to be a pastor," Rosa smiles. "He already is one," I tell her.

With characteristic modesty, Roberto and Rosa leave one vision unspoken. It is their biggest dream. Their friend Bob Vryhof lets me in on it. After we finish lunch and say our goodbyes, Bob tells me, "Their aim is nothing less than a nation of businesspeople on their knees before God."

"There was only lack till I gave my life to Christ."

Santos Apolonia Garcia Lopez

Transformation in the Pulperia

BY TIMOTHY STONER

T he town of Granada nestles on the shore of Lake Cocibolca. Although it bears the honorific designation of the *Gran Sultana del Gran Lago*— the Great Sultan of the Great Lake—it is now more sullen than sultan. Granada was established in 1524 and holds the distinction of being the oldest city founded by Europeans on mainland America. But poverty, decay, and a faltering national economy have not been kind to this town. However, in spite of economic downturns the central cathedral has been lovingly maintained. With its newly painted creamy yellow façade, it reigns over a city of over 100,000 people, most of whom do not have work.

In this town lives Señora Santos Apolonia Garcia Lopez. She invites our group (which included me; Partners Worldwide staff member Lora Kleinsasser and her husband, Joel; and Mario Llanos of Kingdom Business) into her small back yard enclosed by plain cement walls on all sides. The ground beneath our seats is hard-packed dirt, and clotheslines bisect the little compound. As we sit down, Apolonia's husband, without any evidence of chagrin, hospitably unpins his wife's undergarments from the clotheslines to improve the conversational sight lines.

Being prosperous store owners, they ceremoniously bring out cups of cold cola. Drinking them proves to be a complicated and unnerving project, since waves of gnats buzz us perpetually as we talk. One of our group, unaware of the need for caution (meaning a hand over the plastic cup at all times) drinks in

Her only collateral was the four chairs we are sitting on, her bed, and the plastic table used to launch her business.

several uninvited guests on his first swallow. Because I dodge and weave and swat as I drink, my notes are barely legible, but that's no matter; Apolonia's story is unforgettable.

As a young woman, she put herself through nursing school and worked long night shifts for 30 years, receiving barely a subsistence wage. Then in 2003, at the age of 47, a back injury forced her to quit her job. Hers was the only source of family income because at the time her husband and son were drug addicts.

One day her daughter, who owns a medium-size store, provided Apolonia with eight dollars' worth of fresh vegetables and fruit. Rather than eat what her daughter had given her, Apolonia decided to sell it. She set the produce up on a small plastic table in a busy area of town. The fresh food sold quickly. That evening she used the money to buy food for her family and to buy more produce to sell.

For the next two years she managed to eke out a living with her 4'-by-4' plastic fresh-fruit-and-vegetable stand. Then on February 15, 2005, Apolonia became a follower of Jesus. "Almost immediately," she told me, "everything began to change."

Apolonia's story of transformation is so compelling that I drain my cup without realizing it, probably ingesting a few gnats in the process. After her conversion she began praying in faith, trusting that God would bless her business.

Within two months the local banker came to the tiny store Apolonia was now running out of her house and asked if she would be interested in a business loan. Her only collateral was the four chairs we are sitting on, her bed, and the plastic table used to launch her business. Nevertheless, the banker offered to lend her $160.

With this infusion of capital Apolonia added beans, oil, and sugar to her store's stock. She slowly began expanding into other food items. A frugal and wise steward, she decided to purchase a refrigerator to extend the life of the store's produce and to save the cost of ice blocks to keep the soda cold. She announced to her family that they would eat only beans and rice until the refrigerator was paid for.

Kingdom Business

In 2006 Apolonia attended a "Kingdom Business" conference that transformed her understanding of how to run her enterprise. The conference taught her how to organize, budget, keep books, improve customer relations, and manage her time better.

Kingdom Business is one component of the job creation commitment of Partners Worldwide in Nicaragua. It was developed by the Nehemiah Center, an interdenominational ministry hub that brings together nine international mission and development organizations. Joel Huyser, a lawyer from Grand Rapids,

Michigan, codirector of World Missions for Latin America, and a friend of Doug Seebeck, helped establish it.

Mario Llanos, the director of Kingdom Business, is mentored by Jim Tuinstra, who directed Hope Network in Michigan. Together they launched Kingdom Business with the goal of raising up and teaching entrepreneurs in local churches. Cell groups would be formed to train micro-business owners and church members interested in starting small businesses. The curriculum would focus on developing a biblical worldview and integrating kingdom values into one's life and business.

Their vision was to involve a total of 150 participants within three years. Mario began facilitating these seminars in churches from several denominations. Invitations were only by word of mouth. Within 18 months, more than 1,300 people were members of Kingdom Business *nucleos* (cell groups) throughout Nicaragua. Mario reports that "there has been complete transformation in the cell groups' understanding about business management from a Christian perspective."

Apolonia is a member of one of these *nucleos*. After the Kingdom Business conference, she focused on treating her customers with respect and honesty and offering them only the best quality possible. As suggested by the Kingdom Business curriculum, she also asked customers what they wished her store would carry. She began tracking sales to plan her purchasing so these items would be available when needed. In a business context oriented to survival—which looks ahead only as far as the next meal—strategic planning and careful record-keeping are revolutionary concepts.

"I knew God would take care of me. That is what he had promised. He will lead us on to great things!"

As the business grew, Apolonia realized she needed a freezer. Again, money was an issue, but her faith did not falter. "I knew God would take care of me. That is what he had promised," she said. "It is his purpose to bless me and my family. He will lead us on to great things!" Before buying the freezer, as she had done with her new refrigerator, she went to the appliance store and found the one she wanted. In front of the same salesperson, she laid hands on it and proclaimed, "This freezer will be mine!" The clerk smiled and said, "I know—that is what you said before, and you were right." With a bemused smile Apolonia tells us, "People I've never seen in my whole life began coming to my store to buy things." Six months later she had the freezer paid off.

Today, Apolonia is the proud owner of a classic Nicaraguan *pulperia*—a little shop filled with everything imaginable. By Nicaraguan standards, her 8'-by-10' store is luxurious.

When she joined the Kingdom Business cell she was selling 46 pounds of sugar and 80 pounds of rice per month. Her eyes glow contentedly and she smiles widely as she counts on her fingers. Sales have increased exponentially: 700 pounds of sugar and 1,000 pounds of rice per month. She is now also selling about 300 loaves of bread each week and has had to add another employee.

Though it would have been easy, Apolonia did not allow her growing business to become the consuming focus of her life. She tells us that she now volunteers regularly in a women's ministry, takes care of the small children in church, and leads a study teaching younger women to follow Jesus. They make handcrafts, share their problems, and visit the sick together. "Most importantly," she says with conviction, "I teach them to walk in integrity before the Lord." From the financial blessings she has received, she has been able to feed the poor and provide food for the evangelists from her church who travel to remote areas to preach the gospel.

One of the things Apolonia learned from the Kingdom Business conference was the importance of having a group with whom to share the joys and frustrations of running a business. There are eight members in her *nucleo,* or cell. Their purpose is to encourage, pray, celebrate, grieve, and hold each other accountable. They freely share ideas that are working, discuss business practices that are proving beneficial, and talk honestly about difficulties they encounter as Christian business owners. Each of them has attended the conference and is seeing steady expansion with a noticeable growth in sales.

They don't call themselves a church, but that is what they are. When they meet, Jesus is in their midst. He blesses them through the voices and the hands of fellow small business owners in hundreds of cells around Nicaragua. This is perhaps the best thing the *nucleos* have learned: growing a business is good, but being a part of a loving community that is living through the same struggles you are and is committed to your financial and spiritual success is much better.

The Porch

Because of the growth of Apolonia's business and the speed with which she repaid her loans, the bank officer again came to her house offering a loan. This time it was considerably more: 50,000 cordobas ($2,600).

As she tells this, Apolonia's eyes brim with tears and her face beams with overwhelming joy. She points happily toward the wall of the house behind her. Barely able to get the words out now, she tells us that with the second loan she was able to build the cement porch in front of her house. When we came in I hadn't really noticed it. It has an unpainted cement floor and metal posts with a corrugated roof. There are three cement steps leading up to it. It provides cover for the large window through which her customers look in to select the products from her *pulperia*. Though I had paid it no attention when I walked into her house, that porch was the fulfillment of a 30-year dream. It also almost proved her undoing.

The growth of Apolonia's business did not come without opposition. A neighbor was keeping track of the home improvements. She noticed the new refrigerator and freezer, but when the addition to the front of the house was completed, that pushed her over the edge. That was all the proof she needed to justify her suspicions. In her mind, there was only one possible explanation for these "luxury" items and for the speed of Apolonia's upward mobility after decades of poverty. In Granada, you can only get ahead that quickly by selling illegal drugs.

Everyone knew Apolonia's husband was a long-term addict. In town he was a notorious ne'er-do-well. He had contacts and connections in all the wrong places. It seemed obvious to Apolonia's neighbor that something fishy was going on. So the neighbor reported what could only be "criminal" activity going on behind the facade of the outwardly innocent *pulperia*.

Although the leaders of her church were terrified, Apolonia told them not to worry: "The Lord will protect us. He will take care of this." Within a few days, the neighbor came to the *pulperia* crying and asked for forgiveness. She had withdrawn her complaint. God had somehow changed her heart and convicted her of her jealousy and resentment.

God also changed the heart of Apolonia's husband. It started with Apolonia's decision to begin selling soda in her *pulperia*. It was a profitable venture; her eyes glisten when she explains that she makes 15 to 20 cents per bottle. But as a Christian, she knew that she had to honor the Lord with her finances, so she set aside the profits from the first four bottles of soda as a "firstfruits offering." A short while later, her husband and son became Christians, and they are now free from drug addiction.

A Westerner might call that a coincidence. To Apolonia, it was a sign of God's favor. She continues to set aside the initial sales from her soda pop as a firstfruits offering to God. She has learned that her success is dependent on God's grace, not on her own cleverness or abilities. He has blessed her family, and she continues to walk before him in humility, gratitude, and integrity. Her life is not only an example for her community, but for the gringos sitting in a circle in her back yard swatting gnats and learning wisdom.

Nicaragua: Reflections *by Doug Seebeck*

Until the poor have economic freedom, they aren't very free at all. One of Partners Worldwide's fundamental objectives in working with farmers in Nicaragua is to promote a sense of dignity and self-worth through land ownership. Esteban's story perfectly illustrates the effectiveness of the strategy. When the landless become landowners, they also become people who are not objects of charity, but responsible individuals capable of providing for their families and blessing their communities. The goal is to shatter the mentality of inadequacy, passivity, and dependence fostered by well-intentioned programs that subtly communicate, "You can't do it yourselves, so we'll just do it for you."

The hurdles that farmers like Esteban have to overcome are substantial. Volcanic topography is just one of them. The steep mountainous inclines, some as acute as 60 degrees, are an immense challenge. The farmers need education in soil conservation to learn how to protect the little fertile land they have. Cattle have eaten the grass on these mountains for centuries, so besides being impossibly steep, the earth is packed and overgrazed. It requires intensive labor to bring the land back to a state of fertility.

About a year ago I visited a Nicaraguan land bank and was moved to tears by what I saw. The contrast between the farms owned by formerly landless farmers and the farms that were still being rented was amazing. In my lifetime I have walked thousands of farms, but have never been quite as impacted as I was on that particular trip. It is so obvious that Nicaragua's food security lies in providing greater opportunity for more farmers to own the land they work.

But it is not simply economics or culture or geography that keeps the poor in bondage—sometimes it's ingrained attitudes of failure, victimization, inferiority, and inadequacy. Sometimes it's the church itself; many farmers feel condemned for taking loans because their church teaches that Christians should never incur debt.

Zayda Reyes, a trained counselor and one of the directors overseeing land banks, says,

> These bondages control the way the farmers think. They restrict them, preventing them from believing they can actually succeed. They have an inherent expectation of defeat; a mentality of victimization, of poverty, of failure. This attitude inhibits an entrepreneurial spirit, blocking them from moving ahead aggressively. And these attitudes cannot be overcome simply with better farming techniques or more demanding accountability requirements. Clear, better-crafted contracts will not do the job either. What they need most is to learn to destroy these strongholds that are holding them captive to defeat, to failure, to poverty.

Zayda is affirming what I've experienced in Muslim, Hindu, and Christian communities all over the world. When the poor understand that God did not plan poverty, does not intend for them to be poor, and wants fullness of life for them, deep changes begin to happen.

This was Christ's mission, to set the captives free. And this is the mission he gives anyone who says he or she wants to be his disciple and follow him. "Become like me," I believe he is saying, "set the captives free, and if it will require you to break the power of pervasive cultural, spiritual, demonic strongholds, then by all means do that as well."

Reading the stories from these land banks has taught us that the spiritual strongholds in these communities are very deep. They highlight the reality that we are engaged in more than a merely economic, educational, and intellectual battle. We are in a struggle that requires those on both sides of the ocean to be alert and well-equipped in the use of the spiritual weapons Paul tells us are "mighty to the pulling down of strongholds."

Our North American partners, especially, need to faithfully and confidently take up the supernatural weapon of prayer as a vital tool for economic development. For, as Paul admonishes us, "our battle is not against flesh and blood but against the principalities and powers, against the spiritual forces of evil in the heavenly places." These are the forces that also hold the minds of the poor captive to hopelessness and despair and hinder entrepreneurial success. What we are learning is that if we are going to come alongside our brothers and sisters in the developing world and truly ease their burden, we have to better understand the real nature of the battle and how best to fight alongside them.

> When the poor understand that God did not plan poverty, does not intend for them to be poor, and wants fullness of life for them, deep changes begin to happen.

Personal relationships also bring about deep changes. My friends in Africa say that the first time they meet an American they do not see their new acquaintance as a person but as just another *mzungu* ("a person who goes round and round"—a tourist). If the American comes back again, he is a visitor. But when she returns a third time, she is a friend.

We certainly want North American farmers to share their experiences and expertise with Nicaraguan farmers when asked. We also want a component of their partnership to be about evaluating progress. But, more than anything else, we want their visits to celebrate successes and build up the farmers.

This model differs significantly from that of the conventional short-term mission trips. There has been much written lately about the cost benefit of such missional ventures. The best and most comprehensive study I've read was conducted by Kurt Verbeek of Calvin College. He and his wife, Joanne, have worked and lived for many years in Honduras, and lead a semester abroad program there. They initially challenged me on our strategy of having businesspeople come on short visits, so I explained the difference. Our partners, rather than doing a building project and leaving the country for good, work on strategic, long-term partnerships that build capacity, businesses, leadership, and talent to create sustainable jobs far into the future. They usually return to the same place and reconnect with the same people at least yearly.

That's what people like Don and Bonnie Vos are all about, too. Because of their faithful commitment, Don and Bonnie earned the right to share with their Nicaraguan friends their own experiences at a deeper, more personal level. They are able to speak powerfully of their own struggles, discouragements, failures, and their hard-earned successes, too. They are neighbors leaning over the fence letting their friends know that they understand—it has been hard for them as well. They are peers, sweating and struggling together in a demanding, sometimes heart-breaking vocation.

The result of partnerships like these, along with the growth of self-worth and an entrepreneurial spirit of vision and courage, is a new and healthy middle class in Nicaragua. Inch by painful inch they are starting to believe that there is more to life—that it's possible to take off and soar over the mountains like the beautiful macaws. A few see even wider panoramas as they gain a vision for transforming not only their own families, but entire communities.

Apolonia and all the businesspeople Roberto and Rosa Espinosa serve are also deeply connected with the farmers in the land banks. As retailers, they sell the products that come from those farms. But something very important that may not be immediately apparent needs highlighting here. All of the businesspeople and farmers whose stories you've read are members of small accountability and support groups. They meet regularly together for encouragement, accountability, and support, to pray and plan, to teach and share resources. There is nothing more powerful, and that is why this movement is succeeding worldwide.

As these groups extend the compassion of Jesus to each other through the power of the Holy Spirit, the power of their love explodes outward in concentric circles, impacting neighborhoods, communities, cities, and nations, and the world becomes more what God intended it to be. And as those who follow Jesus become known as gracious agents of reconciliation, the light of their good works grows increasingly brighter, bringing not only economic hope and spiritual renewal, but glory to God.

Uganda

The Context

BY DOUG SEEBECK

When Gail and I were about to be posted to Uganda in August 1983, a former colleague from Bangladesh pulled out a map. He put his finger on the small nation on Africa's eastern coast and told me, "Well, at least you're going to a beautiful part of the world. It's near Lake Victoria—the second largest freshwater lake on the planet—located in the east Africa highlands, with decent temperatures. And game parks too." With a sly smile he added, "Just watch out for bullets."

We were going to work with the one million Ugandan refugees displaced by the violence following the overthrow of the infamous dictator Idi Amin. Uganda in those years was one of the wildest places I have ever experienced.

When we arrived at the airport in Entebbe on the shores of picturesque Lake Victoria, we saw armed soldiers everywhere. The airport was riddled with bullet holes, its windows were broken, and most of its lights were not working. It was dark and dingy. Water was not running in the faucets, the toilets were backed up, and a pungent aroma testified that the bathrooms hadn't been disinfected in a good long while.

Beautiful and Terrifying

But as we settled into our new surroundings, we found that Winston Churchill had not exaggerated when he described Uganda as the "pearl of Africa." It was to be our home for four years, but it was both a beautiful and a terrifying place. We soon learned that we had to stay indoors at night, because at night the army would impose martial law and killings would begin. We saw death and destruction up close, and it changed us forever. At the same time, we formed deep friendships with the most gentle and wonderful people we had ever met. But during the four

Winston Churchill had not exaggerated when he described Uganda as the "pearl of Africa," but it was both a beautiful and a terrifying place.

years of our stay, more than 500,000 of their compatriots were killed.

When people think of Uganda, they think of Idi Amin and conclude that he was the root of the nation's problems. As is so frequently the case, the political turmoil was more complicated than that.

The seeds of the conflict were planted by the British when they first discovered Uganda. They were impressed with its geography and its natural beauty. But they were equally impressed with the sophisticated administrative and political infrastructure throughout the kingdoms of the south. After all, where else in Africa could they find kings and queens that so resembled their own?

Instead of colonizing Uganda, as they did in neighboring Kenya, the British made it a protectorate in 1894. At the outset they committed a serious strategic error: they decided that the southern light-skinned Bantus would administer the entire country, while the northern dark-skinned Nilotic warriors would make up the national army. That single decision sowed seeds of division and tribal hatred that resulted in horrible bloodshed many years later.

When Uganda achieved its independence in 1962, Milton Obote, a brilliant northern politician, formed an unlikely alliance with the *kabaka* (king) of the Baganda in the south to form the country's first national government. Obote would be prime minister while the *kabaka* would be president. But it was only a matter of months before the *kabaka* fled to England as a refugee and Obote inflicted the gravest of insults by turning the ornate palace of the king of the Baganda into an army barracks.

The people rejoiced when Idi Amin, an army general from the obscure Kakwa tribe in the northwestern corner of Uganda, engineered a coup in 1971 while Obote was attending the Commonwealth Meetings in Singapore. The people's rejoicing soon turned to weeping, however, when they discovered Amin was anything but a savior.

The general had only a limited education, and wrestling with the challenges of a new young nation overwhelmed him. He impulsively kicked out the country's strong Asian business community and handed their thriving enterprises over to his army comrades. Random killings began, the business sector collapsed, and the people's hope turned to terror.

In February 1986, as we celebrated the birth of our first son, Lucas Mirembe (our Ugandan colleagues gave him the Luganda name for "peace," because when he was born the war stopped) Yoweri Museveni took over the government and normalcy began to return. The deposed and predominantly northern army was driven across the northern border into southern Sudan. But they regrouped with a plan to fight, because when governments are established through armed will, and not by the verdict of the people, those who rise by the gun also fall by the gun.

In a bizarre turn of events, a prophetess named Alice Lakwena, who claimed she was the Holy Spirit, took the leadership of this displaced army and a new resistance began. The rebels marched back toward Kampala, greased with oil that they claimed protected them from bullets. Alice Lakwena was captured near Kampala in October 1987 at the precise time of the birth of our first daughter, Maisha Rae (her Swahili name means "life," because the Ugandan women told Gail it was a gift from God to have a living baby when so many people of all ages were dying).

Everyone breathed a sigh of relief, because now Uganda could move forward, rebuild national unity, and do the hard work of reconciliation. But it was not to be. Alice's cousin, Joseph Kony, assumed leadership in her absence and named the rag-tag rebel group the Lord's Resistance Army.

It wasn't long before money and weapons began trickling in to this group, and the LRA grew to become a ruthless army of murderers that has terrorized northern Uganda for more than 20 years. They rape and pillage at random, swooping in without warning to abduct children and force them to become soldiers or sex slaves. Estimates are that perhaps as many as 30,000 children have been conscripted at gunpoint and degraded into conscienceless killing machines. They are often forced to kill their own parents so they will have no homes to return to.

While the majority of the country flourished and advanced after Museveni came to power, huge areas of northern Uganda deteriorated under the threat of the LRA. Those who visit Uganda often observe that it is as though some areas have reverted to the Dark Ages.

Potential Everywhere

This historical background makes the stories you are about to read all the more miraculous. They are set in the north, the region of Uganda that has suffered so much and for so long.

In March 2003 I hopped on a small Missionary Aviation Fellowship plane from Mwanza, Tanzania, where Partners Worldwide had just inaugurated a new business incubator. I was flying to Kampala to spend a few days with CRWRC field staff. I was interested in a promising new project partnership for the commercial production of a nutritious grain called amaranth. My purpose was to determine whether Partners Worldwide could identify some Ugandan business champions to start a new affiliate.

The more I saw, the more optimistic I became; there was great potential everywhere. I met with Peter Timmerman, CRWRC's team leader, for lunch at an outdoor café in downtown Kampala. When I described the type of businessperson we would need to get started, Peter nodded his head thoughtfully. "I know a few people like that up in Gulu. Let me talk with them," he said.

Thanks to Peter, the following year I met Timothy Jokkene at Partners Worldwide's 2004 conference in Grand Rapids. As you will read, by making this connection Peter did a good thing—a very good thing indeed.

Michelle Jahnke

"Now I don't see anything as impossible."

Timothy Jokkene
Financier to the Poor

BY TIMOTHY STONER

I am spending three days in northern Uganda with a businessman named Timothy Jokkene (pronounced *Jo-keh-neh*). In a country where anecdotal estimates place unemployment near 80 percent, Timothy is an amazing success story. He is a rags-to-riches kind of a guy, except that his riches are not on display. I soon learn that he is piling up treasure, but it is not on this earth. Out of love for Jesus, to whom he has given his life, Timothy is sending his treasure on ahead, where his heart is.

By enabling business start-ups, creating jobs, providing cattle and plows for the impoverished, and caring for hundreds of orphans, Timothy is irrefutable proof that even in the most inhospitable economic climate there is hope. Timothy has embraced the role of mentor, cheerleader, coach, and financier to the poor. "Experience has shown me that a lot of people can make it, they just need someone . . ." —he hunts for the right words, and then hits it on the head—"to kick-start them."

> Timothy is irrefutable proof that even in the most inhospitable economic climate there is hope.

"Life Was Not Easy"

Timothy grew up in a small village in the province of Gulu in northern Uganda. I ask him to tell me a bit about his family context. He explains that his father was a polygamist who had three wives. In 1979 Timothy was preparing to go to university when Idi Amin's removal thrust the country into bloody political and social upheaval. Timothy was not able to pursue his education. At the age of 20 he found work at a Shell gas station in Gulu, which is near Uganda's border with Sudan. He rented a room in a garage and worked at the station for the next six years.

When the rebel coalition that regrouped under the Lord's Resistance Army (LRA) became a growing threat, the new government of President Museveni made a natural assumption. Given the country's history of civil strife between north and south, they assumed that the rebels were receiving sympathy and support from the communities in the north—especially from the people of means and influence.

During this period of suspicion and confusion, the army arrested upwards of 5,000 people in towns across the north, from Timothy's tribe—the Acholis—and the neighboring Langi tribe to the east. Many others were killed, including one of Timothy's brothers who was murdered in front of him. In 1988 Timothy was put in maximum security prison—a facility that would make Guantanamo look like a tourist resort.

When he was finally released, he learned that all 1,000 head of his family's prized cattle had been stolen by marauders on both sides of the conflict. Timothy had lost everything, including four of his uncles who had been killed. He had no income, no assets, no one to welcome him home. Because of the ongoing tribal conflicts it was impossible for him to return home, at least not until hostilities ceased.

"Since there was so much suspicion I had to look for a job in this strange capital city of Kampala to sustain me and my family," he says. By this time he was married and had three children. He found work as a day laborer, off-loading freight trucks in the industrial area of the city. This once-wealthy cattleman was reduced to working for poverty wages. The only housing he could find was a small one-room apartment. During the day it was a kitchen and living room, and at night it was a bedroom for five people. "Life was not easy," he tells me, "especially for someone used to living in the country."

A Unique Opportunity

In 1989 Timothy heard that the CalTex-Chevron gas station across the street from the Shell station where he had worked as a young man had been abandoned. Recognizing a unique opportunity, he approached a Chevron officer in Kampala and offered to purchase the station. Negotiations took several months, but Timothy never lost hope. "Each time they asked me whether I had the money to buy the station, I would tell them, 'Do not worry, it will be no problem.'"

Timothy smiles a bit at his own audacity, because at that time he had only $50 in the bank. But there was more than mere bravado at work. "I knew that God owns all the money and that somehow he would help me get it. So each time they asked me about my resources, God gave me the grace to reply confidently."

Eventually, Timothy and Chevron worked out a purchase agreement and Timothy returned to Gulu to ask the town's only bank for a loan. Years earlier, the banker had taken note of Timothy's honesty in handling the Shell station's money. He trusted Timothy and wanted to lend him the money, yet regulations required him to demand collateral. The problem was that Timothy had only $50 to his name.

The banker decided to bend the rules to provide the initial capital. The loan was just enough to buy 2,500 liters of diesel fuel, 2,500 liters of kerosene, and 2,500 liters of gasoline. Timothy now had product to sell, but no money to pay employees. So he found three unemployed men, including his younger brother, who agreed to work for him for three months without pay. Timothy spent his cash on stationery, a ruler, a pen, and a rubber stamp to make his business documents look official. A borrowed desk and chair completed his office.

> At that time he had only $50 in the bank, but there was more than mere bravado at work. "I knew that God owns all the money and that somehow he would help me get it."

The day Timothy opened the station there was a regional fuel shortage that left his competitors with no gas to sell. Timothy's station sold out in 48 hours. The banker had expected repayment within two weeks, but Timothy paid him back in two days. The officer was amazed. "From now on, Timothy," he told him, "if you need money you come to me, but do not come at the end of the month when it will have to go on the books. Come earlier so you can repay the loan before the books close." Timothy was able to keep his station open and to buy fuel for a year without any collateral.

He received excellent support from the community because they knew and respected him. His station was always filled with customers, even though his prices were not necessarily the lowest in town. "From the beginning, there was a jam from morning till evening. And it is still that way."

His competitors, despite being larger and offering more food products, as well as frequently underselling him, had fewer customers. On our visit to the CalTex station that is now being purchased by his brother, this is proved out. Across the street at the Shell station prices are cheaper but the customers are sporadic. Timothy's station is bustling and its small garage is filled.

I shake my head. "That makes no logical sense," I say. He smiles and nods. It doesn't. "But, it is always like this," he says, indicating the lines that are forming at the pumps. "It is just the favor of God. And the trust." My son, Jonathan, who is with me taking film and photographs, later asks him to sign some release forms. Timothy asks what he is signing and I tell him jokingly that he is signing all his gas stations over to me. I am, after all, a lawyer, and not much of a comic.

In Uganda the odds are stacked so high against small businesses that the slightest success is almost miraculous.

He signs and smiles. "Good. You can have them," he says, as he keeps filling in the forms. "What you take away from me God will give back more." I smile back and think of Abraham and Isaac and Joseph and others in the Scriptures who you couldn't really harm, even if they could be hurt, because the favor of God rested so heavily on them. And I know that this is just another in the long line of such men and women. This one just happens to live in one of the most devastated, impoverished countries in East Africa.

Timothy's next business endeavor was to open a small shop selling consumer goods. After that he purchased additional gas stations. By 2008 he had six stations scattered throughout the nearby districts, and two in the capital city of Kampala. He also owns a soft drink distribution company. When he bought the business in 1991, sales hovered around 500 cases per month. Today, the volume has increased to 20,000 cases per month. This level of expansion is almost beyond belief in northern Uganda, where the odds are stacked so high against small businesses that the slightest success is almost miraculous.

Transportation Troubles

But they have transportation problems, and I soon find out why. Several years ago, an international Christian charity was in need of large transport vehicles to deliver emergency supplies. The charity's local director in Gulu, a friend of Timothy's, asked him for a favor. "Can we use your truck and drivers to deliver bags of food? We want to help those who are starving in the rural areas caught in the middle of the war. It will only be for a brief period," he promised.

Timothy's vehicle was capable of carrying thousands of cases of soda. He had just spent $35,000 to purchase it. But it was uninsured. In war zones, coverage is impossible to obtain and self-insurance is available only if a corporation has large inventories. Timothy was torn. Business logic told him the idea was a very bad risk. On the other hand, his friend was a Christian, directing a Christian NGO, and the need was desperate. Despite grave reservations, Timothy allowed himself to be convinced. The verbal agreement was that his drivers would deliver the food and he would be paid after the goods were delivered.

Over several months, Timothy's drivers made numerous trips for the charity. Then what he had most feared happened. His truck was ambushed by the LRA and was destroyed by a mortar. The driver and his assistant were both killed. Because the goods were not delivered, the relief agency did not pay for the trip. They offered the barest of apologies and, because no contract had been signed, refused to pay for a replacement. Timothy was left without the means to transport his products to his markets.

Now, several years later, Timothy still has not been able to afford to purchase a large transport vehicle. He is forced to lease a truck whenever he brings in a large shipment from Kampala. I am furious and I tell him so. He shrugs his shoulders. "There have been maybe five or six directors since then. There is no one who you could speak with. There was no contract." He chalks it up to experience. It is a hot, humid day. I am getting a lot hotter.

Timothy smiles patiently at me. I tell him I want to do what I can to see that justice is done. But who to talk to? I want to take violent action, but what I want to do most of all is beg the forgiveness of my humble, incredibly generous brother for our arrogance, for those in the West who claim to be the face of charity but live, oh so well, off poverty. I seethe in frustration. I comfort myself that there will come a day when the last will, in fact, be first and that sweet justice will be dispensed and enjoyed forever.

One Job Feeds Five People

At the time of our conversation Timothy was in the process of selling his gas stations to his employees. He is 50 years of age and is getting too old to make frequent trips that take him away from his family for days on end. After all, traveling in this part of the world is not like zipping along on a sales trip, multi-tasking with your Blackberry, hopping from one appointment to the next, Starbucks cup never far from hand. The 210-mile trip from Kampala where Timothy and his family live to Gulu where two of his gas stations are located is a physically and mentally draining six-hour ride.

> Running his own business has transformed his life and enabled him to help transform the lives of thousands.

Most of the time is consumed dodging potholes that would swallow an economy-size vehicle and utterly unbrace a larger sedan. Axles of the unwary can be snapped like dry tinder. The motion inside the driver's compartment is an exhausting series of fits and jerks. Your body is thrust back and forth with the torturous acceleration and deceleration. It is a merciless, sometimes dangerous, unsynchronized, meandering game of dodge-the-holes.

So Timothy is ready to put those stations in someone else's hands. He is a firm believer in the entrepreneurial spirit and the dignity of having a business of one's own. He views himself as a testament of what is possible for many. Running his own business has transformed his life and enabled him to help transform the lives of thousands.

As an example, Timothy tells me the story of Aloysius Kongoli, an orphan from Kampala. When Aloysius was 14 years old he lost both his father and mother to AIDS, leaving him to care for three younger siblings. Sadly, this situation is all too common. Timothy tells me he himself provides for nearly 40 orphans from his extended family alone. But Timothy was moved to help Aloysius. He says, "I told Aloysius that I could not promise to pay his school fees, but if he was willing to learn a trade I could help him do that."

The orphan boy decided to become a tailor. When he completed the course, Timothy gave him a sewing machine as a graduation gift. He also paid rent on a small space for six months and continued to mentor the young tailor for the next six years. Aloysius is now 25 years old, has a thriving business with eight sewing machines and 10 employees, and is able to send his three siblings to school.

In Africa they say that one job feeds five people. If that's true, then more than 50 people receive their daily bread from Timothy's initial investment of trade school fees and a sewing machine.

In addition to helping orphans, Timothy was using his own savings to provide start-up capital for small businesses. At the outset, he had no organization, no plan, no method. His strategy was to find hardworking people he felt he could trust and lend them money at no interest to get them started.

Although this practice helped many budding entrepreneurs, it almost swamped Timothy. All the records were kept in longhand in receipt books without the help of Excel or Office Pro. Since he was already running several large enterprises of his own it soon became overwhelming. Timothy recognized that if he did not establish some kind of loan institution he would be forced to stop.

"I Had Found My Right Place"

In 2004 Peter Timmerman, the Uganda team leader for CRWRC, introduced Timothy to Partners Worldwide. Timothy decided to attend one of the organization's conferences in Grand Rapids, Michigan. There, he says, "my whole thinking was totally changed." He recalls that the first impact of the conference was "overwhelming relief." A huge weight lifted when he discovered that he was not the only Christian committed to providing a financial hand-up to the poor.

Aloysius Kongoli at his business

At the conference he also realized that for the Christian entrepreneur, business and mission are one and the same. "I had found my right place," he says, "because as much as I wanted to do business as a mission, it had never occurred to me that a businessman can actually minister in his own business by using it as a calling to minister to God. It wasn't until that conference that I understood it."

A huge weight lifted when he discovered that he was not the only Christian committed to providing a financial hand-up to the poor.

Timothy also learned how to make his loan program sustainable. Up to that point he had been treating the microloans more like charity. Through conversations and lectures he learned about efficient systems to track the loans and came to understand that charging interest was the only way to ensure his loan program's continuance and expansion.

This new perspective freed Timothy to launch the microenterprise company he calls Talanta Finance—Microfinance Trust. The name was carefully chosen; it refers to the story Jesus told of those who invested their talents wisely and those who did not. A simple sign outside the unassuming, two-story facility summarizes its purpose: "Promoting your talent in business." Initially it was funded solely by Timothy. Then a Norwegian missionary heard of his work and helped raise $30,000.

In 2006, Rob Tribken, president of Bestfresh Foods in California and one of Partners Worldwide's North American team leaders, visited Uganda with his son John on a Partners Worldwide exploration trip. Rob tells me that helping entrepreneurs gives him great joy. "While it may not sound terribly spiritual, I don't like to talk about my *obligation* to help the poor. I just think it's a lot of fun," he says. He is convinced that "entrepreneurs are building the future." They identify the opportunities and the needs. "Our job," he says, actually restating Partners Worldwide's mission statement, "is to help them succeed." Rob is so committed to the task of raising up businesspeople who are (in my terminology) "missioneurs," he has recently established The Center for Faith and Enterprise to help Christians connect their faith with their business. He was also delighted to become a mentor to Timothy.

As a result of that partnership, Rob decided to personally lend funds to Talanta. What Rob finds so compelling is that Talanta is not only trying to teach the value of hard work and integrity but also the virtues of thrift and saving. Every client who receives a loan is strongly encouraged to save money. Talanta holds the savings, and with the support of the affiliate and the Partners Worldwide Global Fund, the savings are tripled. Thus, every dollar saved becomes three dollars available for loans. The repayments pour into a revolving fund to help more entrepreneurs. At the end of the year the excess is distributed to the members as dividends.

By any standard, Talanta has been incredibly successful. Four years after its inception it has helped start about 1,000 microbusinesses with loans averaging $150, and 200 small businesses with loans averaging $1,000.

With Partners Worldwide's help, Talanta is also getting into the cattle business. In Uganda, Timothy explains, "cattle is almost everything. It is wealth, it is a source of esteem, because the more cattle you have, the more wealthy and more recognized in the community you are. It is what brings you a wife. Without cattle you wouldn't get one. If you have cattle, you have food, your children can marry, your children can go to school. What more do you need?"

Talanta's "Oxen Traction" program is an elegantly simple but revolutionary idea. Through its loan program, Talanta provides two oxen and a plow to two families living in an IDP (Internally Displaced Persons) camp because of attacks by the LRA. That simple action can change two families' lives forever. Timothy explains that it takes three people 30 days to cultivate an acre of land by hand. With the oxen and plow it takes only two days. Timothy estimates that a family could earn 40,000 shillings, or $20, from tilling a field. In Uganda that is serious money.

What is so compelling to Timothy is that this is a practical means of reintegrating villagers back to their homes. He is so committed to this work that he has launched another private initiative: a "restocking" project. Timothy is purchasing cattle, treating them for disease, breeding them for improved quality, and then selling the hybrid calves at a very low profit. Since most people in the camps have no money, he is giving them the calves and allowing the farmers two years to repay the $200 from the income their farms begin to generate. To date, 200 calves have been provided.

Rob Tribken and Timothy Jokkene

"Otherwise these people would never be able to own anything," he says. It is his way of helping out the community "a bit." But it is more than that. "It is my way of saying thanks to God."

There are no programs that excite Timothy more than these, because they are the most effective means of re-establishing the Acholi culture. They also show the greatest promise of breaking the spirit of passivity bred from decades of NGO handouts. The Oxen Traction initiative and the restocking project are pathways back to self-reliance and the dignity of hard, honest work on one's own land.

Timothy estimates that a family could earn 40,000 shillings, or $20, from tilling a field. In Uganda that is serious money.

Following that Partners conference in 2004, Timothy decided to spearhead another local initiative by starting a business affiliate of Partners Worldwide. It is called Ugandan Christian Business Partners (UCBP). If imitation is the most sincere form of flattery, then it would seem that Timothy is not exaggerating the positive influence of Partners Worldwide. UCBP now has more than 86 members—all business owners—from the north and south of Uganda. Thus, among this group of Christian business owners, there is more than business going on—ancient tribal divisions are also being healed.

I am not surprised by the criteria for membership; it is precisely what you'd expect from a man like Timothy. Besides the obvious involvement in business, UCBP members must be "responsible enough to think about bringing others up and not about being a big chief." They work in partnership with Karin Children's Medical Center, a community-based charitable organization that Timothy and his nephew's fiancée, Hope Okeny, founded to provide medical and mentoring services for at-risk women and children. Their services are provided at minimal cost, and many of those helped are victims of HIV/AIDS.

A Rare Compassion

Despite his business acumen and strong commitment to efficient procedures and to honoring commitments, Timothy manages to find a compassionate and difficult balance. "Take a poor widow who has several children," he explains. I detect in his voice a real sadness and an empathy born out of deep experience with suffering. "She has barely enough to feed her family. She borrows some money from us and one of her children becomes ill. She must choose. She must use the money for her business and let her child suffer or die, or pay for bus tickets to the hospital that is five hours away. Arriving there she must wait for hours or days, pay the doctor, and come home."

He looks into my eyes. "What do you do?" The poor woman, without a husband to help, uses the loan to pay for the costs of her child's health care. "Can you blame her for that?" he asks, rhetorically. "What if your brother dies and suddenly leaves you with five children to take care of? If you could barely feed your own family before, what would you do with the business loan?" Timothy is not speaking in the abstract. He has had to navigate these waters scores of times. "We try working with them; sometimes it means more money. We hope it does not happen again." But, he admits, Talanta has occasionally suffered losses. "Some of the loans are not recoverable."

Nonetheless, the vast majority of the microloans are being paid back. Only about 3% are in arrears. That excellent rate is due to the dedication of the loan managers, who regularly visit the homes as well as the businesses of the microenterprise clients. They want to know early on what are the conditions in the family and how they can work together to encourage repayment.

> "The poor woman, without a husband to help, uses the loan to pay for the costs of her child's health care. Can you blame her for that?"

Timothy explains that their strategy is not to chasten borrowers or beat them over the head with the biblical mandate to repay obligations. There is a fine balance needed here. I try to think about how Jesus would treat a widow who got behind on her repayment schedule. I tend to think he would act a whole lot like Timothy.

Bigger Dreams

As our conversation comes to an end, Timothy tells me, "I am thankful for Partners Worldwide because when I met Peter I was very frustrated." People were taking advantage of Timothy, thinking he was helping out because he had limitless surplus. Joining forces with others who have the same heart helped him continue and expand beyond what he had thought possible. With the encouragement of Rob Tribken and others in the Partners Worldwide network to walk alongside him and help bear the burden, Timothy has begun to dream even bigger dreams.

He envisions Talanta Finance becoming a commercial bank. His desire is to spread out the risk, expand the opportunity for savings, and provide larger loans while charging lower interest. It will take one billion shillings (about $500,000) on deposit to make his dream a reality, but he is not concerned or anxious.

"There's really nothing impossible with God. That is the way I look at it. When I started my first business, I had nothing. It was just basically trust. Now I'm running six to seven small enterprises and am able to employ over 100 people. So now I don't see anything as impossible. Of course this did not happen without the help of others. Someone had to have trust in me and push me forward. And even now I have partners overseas. It's not only one person. There are many, and I believe that the dream will come true, without any doubts."

Although he is very thankful for his international partners, his gratitude is mainly vertical. "I have seen what God can do and how lives can be changed. And I want to play my part." I try telling him that he is already doing so much more than most people, but I falter. It is not every day you get to sit next to someone with such humility, dedication, and single-mindedness. I wonder how North Americans measure up.

"I have seen what God can do and how lives can be changed. And I want to play my part."

I pray that Timothy's example will be multiplied a thousand-fold and that the church of Jesus Christ will become notorious for good works of compassion and radical generosity. I pray that I, like Timothy, whose name I share, may do more too.

Larry Doll

Hope Okeny

Driven to Compassion

BY TIMOTHY STONER

I n the 1970s Uganda was a dangerous place to live—especially if, like Prof. Isaac Ojok, you came from the Acholi or Lango tribes in the north.

In 1971, the year that Hope Ojok was born, the brutal and mentally unstable dictator Idi Amin engineered a coup, forcing President Milton Obote, a Langi, to flee the country. At the time, Hope's family was living in Gulu, their family's home for generations. Isaac Ojok was a college professor, teaching at Makerere University in Kampala, Uganda. Hope's mother, Kevina Waigo, taught Braille in a primary school in Gulu. She would later become a successful businesswoman. Hope is the eldest of three sisters and one brother. But the family grew to 11 when six nephews and nieces were informally adopted after their parents died.

I am with Hope walking the streets of Gulu, her hometown. She speaks with the precision and careful intonations that give away the fact that for 10 years she lived and studied in England. She has the energy of a 20-year-old, and her eyes shine with focused intelligence. Though she is unhurried in her conversation, she keeps moving. She is a woman with much on her mind and much to accomplish. I find out later that my estimate of her age is off

Now I see why I am racing to keep up. Hope is not only bright, competent, and successful—she is also driven.

by almost a decade. She is married, has two biological children, and has "adopted" about a dozen more.

With one sentence Hope sketches out for me what being raised by her professor father was like. "Even recently, after I completed my degree (an MBA), Dad asked me if I was just stopping at only a master's." She smiles slightly. "It's kind of in the blood. My uncle once said to me that there is no substitute to education—he himself was a judge then." She continues and it all begins coming together. "Sometimes you just feel like you have one degree and everyone around you has two."

Now I see why I am racing to keep up as we stride along the dusty streets of Gulu. Hope is not only bright, competent, and successful—she is also driven.

Learning Hard Work

Idi Amin, like King Herod of old, was an undiagnosed paranoid psychotic who controlled the nation by terror and murder. His plan was to kill all the educated people, whom he perceived to be a threat to his monomaniacal authority. Since Hope's father had joined the opposition party, things were doubly dangerous for him. In 1977, to avoid being killed by Amin's death squads, Hope's father fled to southern Africa. Hope's mother and the children moved to Kampala.

To make ends meet, Hope's mother started a supermarket in Kampala when Hope was 7 years old. It was called Alabama Stores. Hope tells me that there was no significance in the choice of the name; somewhere her mother had taken a fancy to the sound of that southern U.S. state and chose it for her first business venture. Under her skilled administrative hands the store grew rapidly until it had six employees. Hope was attending a boarding school in Kampala and spent holidays and vacations working in the store. From childhood, all four children were taught the virtue of work. "By the age of 5 I could do most of the housework," Hope explains. "My mum encouraged us to wake up early. We were brought up to work hard. We learned that for us to be successful, it's hard work."

Hope's mother had to make frequent trips into Kenya to purchase packaged goods as well as the majority of other products sold in her supermarket. "When we were young and our mum had to travel, before she left she would tell us that it was our job to count the money every evening." Later, on holidays from the boarding school, Hope would accompany her, learning the skills of bargaining, negotiation, and balancing books. At the age of 12 Hope was placed in charge of the store. For five years she helped her mother manage the successful supermarket, selling high-end products not readily available in other stores.

Ms. Waigo taught her children more than business skills, however. Besides taking in six orphans, Hope says, "she also helped a lot of other children. My mum paid up so many children's fees and all that." The "all that" covers a lot of ground, including uniforms, books, and other expenses of an African education. This is the informal, extended-family social security net that catches some African orphans, but by no means all.

In 1979 things changed again for Hope's family when Idi Amin was forcibly removed by Tanzanian forces aided by Ugandan exiles, including ousted President Obote. He regained the leadership of Uganda in 1980 after questionable elections that led to a guerilla rebellion known as the Bush War. Prof. Ojok was asked to return to his country to serve as Minister of Education.

In 1986, Yoweri Museveni, the current president, came to power through another military coup. Since Prof. Ojok had been a part of the Obote regime, he was arrested in 1988 on trumped-up charges of treason and locked up at the national prison in Luzira for seven years. During the period of his incarceration the family sought legal assistance and Prof. Ojok was eventually cleared of all charges and released. But after the arrest, remaining in Uganda was no longer an option. Ms. Waigo moved her family to England. Hope stayed behind to finish high school, joining her mother in London after graduation.

Uganda Calls

Hope's years in Britain molded her into an emotionally restrained person, but it was her father's absence that shaped her into a tough-minded, independent woman. Even when her father was back in Uganda, Hope explains, he was frequently away. "My father was hardly there with us. During Obote's government he was around, but because of his political position he was always in and out of the country." She gives me an interesting insight into the life of the family of a high-level diplomat. "From childhood it's always been like us travelling to find him, maybe in Nairobi or something. We grew up knowing he was somewhere out there, but they would never tell us why he was away."

However, the impact on the family when Prof. Ojok was imprisoned was worse. Hope was 17 years old at the time. "It was tough on us," she admits. Her father's imprisonment "changed our status from having great respect and dignity, to living in oblivion." That's one of the reasons they were forced to move to England. "It was not safe," she adds, "and we were never sure what would happen to us or my mum. We had these people coming over all the time and asking a lot of questions. It was very scary for us kids."

For Hope, a romantic teenager, the trip to London was more of a lark than an exile. She and her siblings were excited to travel to one of the great cosmopolitan centers of Europe. But as we talk she looks back on that time with different eyes. "My mother just recently told us she'd sit in the apartment bedroom alone and just cry. I told her, 'No wonder you used to close yourself in your room!'" There is regret in Hope's voice as she admits, "I now understand and I feel very bad, but we were too young at that time for her to come and tell us all her disappointments. It would also break us down."

Ms. Waigo courageously battled through her emotional pain and started a small export company. She also opened a hair-dressing salon with three employees. Jolly's Salon did well among the African community and helped provide Hope's tuition at the University of East London.

In 1990, Hope met Julius Okeny, a Ugandan. He was studying law at Liverpool University. Thirteen years later, they married. In 1996 Hope graduated with a degree in business administration and was hired at Ilford Securities, a sister company of the London Stock Exchange. During the Christmas holidays a year later she decided to visit her homeland. It had been almost 10 years since she'd been back.

A Shattered Country

Hope had been reading reports about the civil war in the north, and had been following the bloody exploits of the Lord's Resistance Army. She knew that thousands had died, villages had been razed, and hundreds of thousands of people had been forced to take shelter in internally displaced people (IDP) camps in the region where she was born.

When she arrived in Uganda, the situation was actually much worse than she could have imagined. She met with Timothy Jokkene, the maternal uncle of Julius, her fiancé. Timothy had lived and worked with Julius's parents in Kampala for several years before starting up his own business. As she talked with Timothy and with other people, she says, "Their stories broke my heart."

Hope tells me one particularly shattering story told to her by a child soldier. Eleven-year-old Simon and his younger brother had just returned home for their school holidays. Their father, who raised pigs for a living, asked them to take one pig to market. As the boys were going to get the pig, a group of 20 rebels surrounded the family's home. Simon and his brother tried to escape, but they were captured. The rebels then told Simon to set the house on fire. He resisted, knowing that his family was in the hut. Simon was beaten until he complied. He set the hut on fire and was forced to watch as his parents and his sisters burnt to death. The rebels forced him to become a child soldier.

"This story breaks my heart to this day," says Hope. "I could not listen any further and I remember breaking down and crying uncontrollably. Even Timothy was broken. But we decided to continue listening because we saw a small boy who was equally broken but wanted forgiveness. He wondered if God could ever forgive him for killing his parents and siblings and other members in the community (he even killed many more when he became a child soldier). This boy needed help. Timothy and I prayed with him before we had to leave."

Hope returned to her comfortable flat and stimulating job in England. But she was weighed down with sadness and with images of shattered families and unimaginable physical and emotional suffering. She had been tagged as a "high flyer" with potential to move rapidly up the executive track of England's Stock Exchange. But for six long months she battled within herself, unable to suppress the painful stories she'd heard and the conviction that there was something she could do to alleviate their poverty. One question burned in her mind: "How

One question burned in her mind: "How can I help?"

can I help?" Finally, she could ignore it no longer. She decided to follow her heart and return to Uganda to help her people.

In her supervisor's office her plans tumbled out of her. His response was startling: "Hope," he told her, "you stay as long as you need to, but when you return you will still have a place with us." Before she left for Uganda, the employees of Ilford Securities and Hope's friends collected loads of used clothing for Hope to give to the children of Gulu.

Gulu was nothing like she remembered. It was now a ravaged and destitute city.

Back in Uganda, Hope and Timothy Jokkene travelled to Gulu, leaving early in the morning to make sure they arrived before the military curfew at 6:00 P.M. "I was praying constantly," Hope says. "I did not know if we would make it." As they crossed into the northern provinces they passed blackened trucks that had been hit by explosives and were still smoking. She describes seeing a dented helmet lying along the road. Nobody needed to tell her that they had just missed being ambushed by rebels.

What was most striking were the empty fields without crops, devoid of the characteristic sounds of thousands of head of cattle that had once dominated the land. Though she tried to steel herself for what she would find when she reached her hometown, it was still a shock when they arrived. Gulu was nothing like she remembered. It was now a ravaged and destitute city.

The first place she went to visit was the house where she had grown up. When the home was being constructed by her grandfather in the 1950s, it caused quite a stir because it was one of the first built in the Western style, with iron sheeting on the roof and brick walls rather than reed. When Hope drove up, her heart sank. The beautiful house had been demolished. The sheeting was gone and all that remained were bricks smashed and scattered about the property.

Hope had brought three bags of lollipops to give to the children. With no place to go, they were milling about everywhere. It was the rainy season, the coldest time of year, and the children were clutching their bodies to keep warm. As she began handing the lollipops out, within moments she was being swarmed by hundreds of children desperate to grab the candy from her hand. The ground was muddy and Hope was knocked off her feet. She realized suddenly that she was in danger of being trampled. It was terrifying. "It was like being attacked by animals," she remembers.

She was saved by local camp leaders who heard the commotion. When Hope had cleaned the mud off her clothes as best she could, they explained to her that many of the children had not eaten for days and were close to starvation. Scores had been walking for miles looking desperately for shelter. Naively, Hope had almost provoked a deadly food riot. "You need to learn what not to do here or they will kill you," the camp leaders warned her.

> It was easy to convince herself that there was nothing she could do to make a difference. But she continued to pray for direction.

"You can't imagine what we are living like," they continued. "As far as the government is concerned, we are no better than the scum of the earth. There is no food. Children are being abducted and this has caused so much fear and hopelessness among parents and the community at large."

The leaders explained that they lacked the most basic medicines. All the health workers in the area had fled for their lives into larger towns. The people had no access to clean water, and they feared they would be abducted by the rebels if they traveled far from the camp. Their only recourse was to wait for the rains and collect standing water from holes dug in the ground.

It was very quiet driving back to Kampala the next day. Hope and Timothy began to pray for God to show them how they could serve these people. Hope returned once again to London, carrying a heavy burden for her people. The longer she thought over what she had seen and the atrocious stories she had heard, the more impossible the task became. It felt "too much" for her. The depth and the scope of the needs dwarfed her abilities. It was easy to convince herself that there was really nothing she could do to make a difference. But she kept her pact with Timothy and continued to pray for direction.

The Birth of CDO

After many unsuccessful attempts to get financial support to help Hope's people in northern Uganda, she and Timothy decided to establish Childcare Development Organization Uganda (CDO). Timothy would be its chairman, and Hope the executive director. A needs assessment indicated that children were the most affected by the civil war, and providing help for them would result in the broadest community impact. It also revealed that there were thousands of children who were either abandoned, displaced, or malnourished. What was most tragic was that many of them had been abducted and forced by the LRA to become child soldiers.

CDO began as a relief organization providing food, clothes, and medicine. For several years Hope commuted back and forth between her job in London and her relief work in Uganda.

Since childhood Hope had been intrigued with the idea of being an entrepreneur like her mother. In 2001 she decided to leave England to devote herself fully to CDO and to establishing businesses with her fiancé, Julius Okeny. Their first venture together was a gas station. Two years later Hope and Julius were married. But Hope wanted to do more for herself and for others, so she enrolled in an MBA program. She explains what motivated her. "I wanted to be an entrepreneur

because the people around me have all been entrepreneurs, and from the time I was doing my course I wanted to run a big business. Managing my own business has been my passion. I wanted to be the one in control. Even in school I held leadership positions, but I've always wanted to run a business myself and grow big."

A few years later the Okenys bought an 18-room guest house. Recently they also started a catering company and a company that manages commercial property. These businesses provide jobs for around 30 people.

In May 2005 CDO opened Karin Children's Medical Centre, named after one of the missionaries from Norway who provided the initial financial support. The medical center supported Gulu's children with general medical services such as immunization, as well as family planning for mothers, laboratory testing, and counseling. It has impacted thousands of children in the community.

In 2007 Rob Tribken of Partners Worldwide sponsored a "Christmas market," selling Ugandan handcrafts to raise money for a new medical center. Sales and donations raised close to $8,000. That provided the funds to buy land, equipment, and medicines to open a small clinic in a remote rural area where health services are scarce. This medical center provides immunizations, blood testing for malaria and HIV, and trauma counseling for adults and children. Currently there are two counselors and five full-time staff working for these centers. About 500 children, all of whom have been impacted or traumatized by the incessant hostilities, are being taught peacemaking and life skills.

The Karin clinic provides classes for men, women, and children. The women receive counseling and are taught new skills in cooking and craft making. "They learn to start rebuilding their lives even during times of adversity," Hope explains. "Many women have lost their loved ones in the war. Some have had their children abducted and have no hope of ever seeing them again. They come and share their experiences and this is good therapy for them."

The children come to play because it is safe and their parents trust the workers. It has become an oasis of peace for a community devastated by war. It draws the whole family. Parents come in the evenings to watch their children playing happily together or competing in sports.

I can read both pain and pleasure in Hope's face. "This is something many have not done for years and years. They have been hiding in the bush and living in fear for so long."

More than 20 women are involved in adult literacy classes. They are also being taught how to count their money when doing business. From this class was formed the Karin Parents' Group, a community of entrepreneurs who were taught how to save and borrow money wisely to run their businesses.

When a brother or sister from North America demonstrates sincere interest and a willing heart to serve, it provides a level of encouragement that is hard to measure.

The Parents' Group has started vegetable growing projects to subsidize their businesses. Today the group has over 200 members. It now includes farmers who have been taught modern farming techniques and have received dairy heifer cows and oxen. These farmers are eagerly anticipating being able to provide milk for their families and starting to farm once again when the rainy season begins.

The members who are entrepreneurs were introduced to Talanta Finance and have begun actively borrowing and growing their businesses. They organize themselves into groups of five and agree to stand behind the loans that are taken out. There are now 85 members in this group of entrepreneurs.

"If it weren't for Partners Worldwide we would never have met people like Rob Tribken," Hope adds. Rob's genuine interest, as much as his financial support, has had a profound impact. Hope's comment underlines something American partners find difficult to grasp: the simple, unimaginable power of coming alongside others.

Business in the developing world—and life in general, for that matter—is so difficult, and the barriers so exhausting, that when a brother or sister from North America demonstrates sincere interest and a willing heart to serve, it provides a level of encouragement that is hard to measure. "We are working with a community that is coming from nothing," Hope tells me, "all of us need guidance." What she is saying is that the needs here are limitless. While the challenge can be paralyzing, it need not be, for even small contributions can provide substantial, life-changing impacts.

As a result of the support from Rob and Partners Worldwide, Hope says, "We have moved from thinking about just a small clinic to thinking big. Because we believe there is now a 'big brother' that we can call and get ideas from, someone who you can ask for help. And Rob has been that kind of person, at least to me." She then reiterates what I've heard from many others. "The need is more about mentorship, because I really don't think money is what we need. If we had the help to know what we were doing, we would do a lot better."

Though money is not the most vital need, it has had positive outcomes. "The matching funds from Partners Worldwide have made possible small loans that have brought noticeable improvement to the entrepreneurs." These microloans range from $25 to $50. Hope tells me that some of the recipients have used the money to buy bicycles for transportation, "and that has made them actually believe they can do something and run businesses." This is a huge leap forward for someone with a dream but no positive expectations for the future.

Building an Incubator

Perhaps the task that takes most of Hope's energy in Gulu is Uganda Christian Business Partners (UCBP), which she has been managing since she helped organize it in 2006. The idea was planted by Timothy Jokkene, who called her following the Partners Worldwide conference he had attended in Grand Rapids, Michigan. He suggested that they would use Partners' model to grow businesses and develop Ugandan entrepreneurs. So UCBP began with 18 members.

Hope's title is executive secretary, but she wears many hats. The weight of the organization lies mostly on her competent managerial and administrative shoulders. She helps develop and review business plans, mentor small business owners, and assist in setting up projects. Currently, most of UCBP's 86 members are small businesses, around 10 are medium-size, and seven have more than 100 employees. There are almost 30 who are saving up to pay the fees so they can join. The vision is to set up cells in each major city.

Giving so much of her time to help the poor in Gulu has been costly. Hope travels the road leading north from Kampala (a six-hour drive) an average of twice a month, but the trips are often more frequent. "Sometimes I'm here every week or even stay a whole month depending on what's going on." Her commitment runs deep. "It's so difficult to leave these people to do things on their own," she admits ruefully, speaking out of compassion but also out of her admitted need to keep control.

Being away has forced family and business sacrifices. Julius has had to bear more of the weight of running their businesses than he otherwise would want. Though Hope is gone from home a lot, they keep in regular contact by phone, much of it troubleshooting, or, as she calls it, "problem solving." They speak to each other around 10 times a day. But phone conversations are not the same as being there.

Although Hope is reticent to share much detail, she mentions in passing that she and Julius have donated personal funds at various times to keep CDO afloat. Funding has been a great challenge, as has getting the organization on a sustainable footing. In a devastated city like Gulu few can afford to pay for medical services.

One of the income sources are the members of UCBP, who have helped fund the construction of the clinic on the new site and who pay for the services that they receive from the clinic. Other members have been there to help with advice.

"All From Our Heart"

Hope admits that she struggles with disappointment when donors decide not to provide needed funds. On one occasion supporters from Europe came in during the rainy season, and she showed them the hundreds of people who did not have access to any structures to protect them from the elements. Hope explained to them that CDO wanted to construct very simple shelters that would provide significant benefits for these vulnerable members of the community. The cost would be minimal.

"But they didn't fund the project," she tells me. The lines along the side of her mouth are just a little taut. Her frustration is palpable. Walking past the ramshackle dwellings that pass for houses on both sides of the dirt road, the cause of her frustration is obvious. Every day she has to face the pain of hunger, sickness, despair, and death. What she finds most troubling is how essential funding can be denied by fellow Christians who have the means to meet such clear needs.

"You will not see us stop here. These are our people and we are not going to stop helping them!"

I really don't have a good answer for her. There is no simple response. There are limits to financial support. And I could argue convincingly that sustainability is frequently impeded by charitable gifting. But in areas of the world like northern Uganda, which has faced over 20 grinding years of systematic pillaging by vicious soldiers without conscience, you can only move toward that place of self-support after mercy has pulled you back from the brink of death.

Hope continues, interrupting my ponderings, and the needle of conviction is driven deeper. "I remember thinking at that time, I don't think we will fail to do something for our people. If the donors only come in to help in certain situations whatever it is—that's OK. But," and here she shares her unspoken monologue when the donors declined, "I tell you, you will not see us stop here. These are our people and we are not going to stop helping them!" She pauses for a fraction, then continues. "We moved on," she tells me.

After the disappointing response she acknowledges that it would have been easy to conclude that because they didn't get the money the project was dead in the water. But she points to the frail and simple structures that line the road. "A lot of these things you see are things I've put in myself," she says, "it's all from our heart."

Well-deserved Praise

Although she was raised in privileged circumstances, Hope was very aware of the pain of the poor that surrounded them. "I think that as a young girl I always looked around and saw so many people suffering." She also had a mother who modeled compassion and generosity. "I was raised in a Christian family and the Christian schools I attended molded servitude as a Christian into us."

Though she was a sensitive child with good examples, it was her Christian conviction that compelled her to devote so much of her time to serving those in need. It also has given her a hopeful perspective about the possibility of social and economic change. "Being a Christian, I feel that people can always live a different lifestyle if they change their mindset from thinking that they're poor to doing something positive to improve their lives."

> "It's not always that high lifestyle. You can have all that, but what's the meaning of it if you can't help the people around you?"

Julius and Hope have two children, Jordan and Jorgina, but they have also taken upon themselves the responsibility of caring for others. She estimates that over the years they have helped close to a dozen children by paying for their school fees and more. Though it is not a legal process, she explains that "you might call it adoption because they come to us when they have problems." It's more like she and Julius are surrogate parents.

Okot Simon, one of the orphans they helped, was a little boy who had escaped from the war in Gulu. They found him wandering the streets of Kampala. The Okenys raised him and paid for his vocational schooling. He is now running his own business. Susan, another of their surrogate children, is a Sudanese girl who at 14 years of age was abandoned by her mother and was left with nowhere to live. She is now one of the most trusted and diligent employees in the Okenys' guest house. Two other girls, Jennifer and Sonia, were educated up to college level until they got jobs. They have since moved on and married.

Adding to the hardship of serving in the north, Hope has faced criticism for her work in a region of Uganda that most people are all too happy to ignore. "Frequently people, when they see me going to Gulu, they wonder what's wrong with me." She smiles as though she sometimes wonders the same thing. "But I look at life in a different way." And now I begin to see what is underneath the compelling drive of this dedicated woman. "It's not always that high lifestyle. You can have all that, but what's the meaning of it if you can't help the people around you?"

This spirit is what moved her to launch CDO. "It began with a question: How can I do something more apart from these businesses? Julius and I can have everything we want with just our own kids. But there are other people I could be helping at the same time in the little way I can do."

Hope and Julius are providing jobs in the businesses they run in Gulu and Kampala. They also have dreams to open up a hotel or bed-and-breakfast in Gulu. They have already acquired the land and have the plans ready to go. She explains that she is looking forward to placing trustworthy managers in charge who can take care of the daily details of running their various enterprises. Her long-term goal is to be freed up so she can become a consultant and write a book about social entrepreneurship and Christianity.

I am struck by the unique status Hope has gained in the community. It is a respect that can be seen as well as heard. When Hope drops by to visit the businesswomen she mentors, they frequently greet her with the highest honor they can give—high pitched ululations that proclaim: "Here is a woman of honor, here is a woman of worth." The sound brings to mind the praises due to a woman of "noble character" described in Proverbs 31. I have watched Hope, and I know the praise is well deserved. She is a woman who loves others as Christ commands us to.

> "When you see how many people's lives have been transformed through our work, how can we stop?"

Persevering in Doing Good

I asked her a final question about the challenges she faces: "What are some of your biggest disappointments?" I am surprised by her honesty. "Wow, there are so many. But I've learned not to dwell on the things that disappoint me. They can depress me so much. I try not to think about it. When you see how many people's lives have been transformed through our work, the number who've sought our advice and are now running their own businesses, the hundreds of children who love to come to the centre even with so little we can provide, as well as all the mothers sitting intently, receiving life-saving health training. How can we stop? They have so much hope in us and they believe in us."

She admits that it is not easy, and there have been times she has been tempted to give up. But then she sees a little child who has been saved from death, or a widow on a path to a hopeful future. She looks into a beaming face that proclaims gratitude and a growing confidence, and she knows she cannot give in. "I choose to turn the disappointments into something productive and beneficial."

Hope has learned to persevere in doing good. She is honoring her Father in heaven and he, I know, is well pleased.

Uganda: Reflections *by Doug Seebeck*

It's difficult to find words for what I am feeling after reading the stories of my dear friends Timothy and Hope. I am troubled by the thought of "what if."

What if Christians from North America or other parts of the world had been willing to go to Gulu to stand alongside Timothy, Hope, and their communities in their time of need? Could the senseless massacres, the outright evil against children, women, and families, have been prevented? What if an army of Christians had arrived in one jet airplane after another at the Entebbe airport, then moved in convoys to the north—not to fight, but to be present, to make a big scene, to expose the evil to the rest of the world?

Gail and I wrestled with this while living in Kampala just before the military coup in 1986. I remember the empty feeling in my guts as we watched the Ugandan military escort a convoy of 500 vehicles full of missionaries, aid workers, and diplomats to the safety of neighboring Kenya before the fighting started in Kampala. Gail and I decided to stay in Uganda then, but we never felt threatened as long as we kept our heads down. We weren't being heroes; neither the rebels nor the government troops were looking to kill U.S. citizens. But we couldn't bear the thought of leaving our Ugandan brothers and sisters behind.

> As Timothy says, "Once you make a decision to follow Christ, to be in The Way, your entire life has to change."

Thank God that Timothy and Hope chose to go back to Uganda to suffer and serve. By doing so they defeated evil and saved the lives of thousands.

Timothy and Hope understand deeply what it means to be servant leaders. It's hard to adequately describe the character and strength of these two people of God. Neither places blame for the troubles of the past, even though there is plenty of blame to go around.

Timothy feels that if God hadn't allowed his herds to be seized, he would never have gone into business. And if he had never gone into business, he would not have been able to help the thousands of people God has placed in his path. What he discovered after venturing into business to survive was that he was an entrepreneur at heart. He was also passionate about serving Christ and using business as a means of blessing others. As Timothy says, "Once you make a decision to follow Christ, to be in The Way, your entire life has to change."

Jesus told his disciples to live a life of sacrificial service, even to the death, and Timothy believed that this command applied to him as well. As a businessperson and a follower of Christ, Timothy could not separate his corporate responsibility from his community commitment. Neither could Hope, which is why she continues to be a driven agent of reconciliation and change in her community.

This underscores the crucial importance of local champions like Timothy and Hope. It might take a while for God to reveal them, but I have come to believe that God places servant leaders everywhere, because that is how his light shines. Rick Warren describes these kinds of leaders as "people of peace," and we are called to find them even if they are not yet Christian, because God works through them.

Similarly, in the business model used by Partners Worldwide, a local champion is also vital on the North American side. It took us three years to find someone in the U.S. who was willing to assume a leadership role for this partnership. While on a trip to Uganda in March 2006, Timothy, Hope, and other business leaders pressed me to get moving and launch a partnership. My heart ached for them as I felt their sense of urgency and discouragement.

Up to that point, we had acted on our foundational principle to have leadership commitments on both sides of the partnership before starting any tactical implementation. It is tempting to move quickly when needs are great, but our dual-commitment principle is one I trust we can continue to maintain because it prevents us from becoming (out of compassion) another NGO in which donors fund a staff of professionals to do the work for them. We do not want to replace these business-to-business partnerships with an organization of "experts" doing the work of ministry in their place. Our goal is to connect, not displace—to empower, not to undermine.

So we waited and we prayed. I was frustrated and, I will admit, just a little angry. I cried out to God, "What's it going to take to get someone to come alongside these folks and encourage them as they rebuild and heal?"

The very next week I received a call from Rob Tribken, the founder and CEO of Best-Fresh Foods in California. He had attended our Business 2003 conference in Pasadena, California, which was co-sponsored by Partners Worldwide and by Fuller Theological Seminary, where Rob was working on his masters of divinity degree. He was writing his thesis on transformational development and wanted to study Partners Worldwide. He asked if I had an hour or two to answer some questions. I agreed, and after our conversation Rob went back to work on his thesis.

A few weeks later, Rob called again. "I don't know why," he said, sounding perplexed, "but for some odd reason, God has been putting Uganda on my heart." Then he asked me the question I'd been waiting for several years to hear: "Do you folks have something going there?" Two months later Rob showed up at our International Business Conference and met Timothy. Before the end of August 2006, Rob and his son landed at the Entebbe airport for the first time. Upon his return, commitments were made to finalize the formation of the Ugandan partnership.

HIV/AIDS and Orphans

As Rob and others on his North America team would soon learn, the challenges of working in Uganda can seem overwhelming. In addition to high unemployment rates, poverty, and corruption, HIV/AIDS has wreaked havoc on this beautiful country.

War and civil unrest, rather than promiscuity, have hastened the spread of AIDS in Uganda, because war uproots people and dehumanizes them. That's painfully clear in the stories of Hope and Timothy and the communities they come from in northern Uganda. In the early 1980s, the north had a very low incidence of HIV/AIDS, while the disease was rampant in the south where the civil war was in full throttle. Currently, the north has HIV/AIDS infection rates as high as 37% in the camps where displaced people have lived for as long as 22 years.

The number of children orphaned by the disease in Uganda is well over one million. While orphanages will always be necessary for some, they should only be a last resort, and a transitional one at that. In African society, placing children in orphanages may condemn them to a life of poverty, because once they are removed from their family's land they have lost the single greatest asset needed for a healthy future. When a country undergoes the extensive crisis that HIV/AIDS brings upon its citizens (especially in concert with war and the destabilization of communities), all types of strategies need to be deployed. But having adopted three Ethiopian orphans who lost their parents in the protracted war during the Mengistu regime, I know that orphans may survive in orphanages, but they thrive in families.

I will never forget our conversation in 1989 with Seble MacKennan from Ethiopia's Ministry of Social Welfare. Her beauty and eloquence did not hide her grief when she said, "Douglas and Gail, we are ashamed that as an African nation we are allowing our children to be taken outside our country. But we are overwhelmed by the number of orphans and the need. Our communities cannot handle this situation alone. So we are thankful that you have come to join and help us." Seble was restating what we had heard many times during our years in Uganda: "In Africa, we will thrive together—or die together."

Timothy's relationship with Aloysius, the young boy he adopted and helped set up as a tailor, is remarkable. Aloysius is Bantu, and light skinned, while Timothy is very dark and is Nilotic. Aloysius is from the tribe that the British appointed as political and economic leaders, while Timothy's tribe was relegated to the culturally inferior military role. Timothy's relationship with Aloysius was a complete reversal and renunciation of hatred bred from subjugation and demotion.

When Aloysius lost both parents, he was taken in by his extended family. He became their indentured servant—but in reality he was their slave. He received one meal per day. He was forced to labor on the farm, and was not given proper clothes. When he describes those years, especially what it was like as an adolescent to wear shorts with large holes exposing his buttocks, he looks down, still ashamed, and his eyes fill with tears. And all the time, he tells me, he was terrified, thinking about what was happening to his younger sisters who had been sent away to Rwanda.

But God was gracious to this orphan boy. He met Timothy at a Christian fellowship in Kampala. Beyond all hope, and against every cultural taboo, this businessman from the north took in a broken southerner and cared for him as his own child. When we spoke about Aloysius, Timothy described him as "a very special boy," and stressed how much his adopted son has blessed him.

And here is the power of leverage. When businesspeople in the U.S. invest in businesspeople like Timothy, Hope, and the other 86 members of the Uganda Christian Business Partners, they are indirectly helping to care for thousands of orphans in a healthy and sustainable way, because most of the members of UCBP are taking care of many children— some relatives, some not—orphaned by HIV/AIDS.

"We want you to fight with us, not for us, in our war on poverty."

Timothy and Hope vividly illustrate the reality that businesspeople motivated by love can radically transform their communities. The impact they have made on those communities is astonishing, especially in a place like Gulu where the majority have lost their means of livelihood and, with it, their dignity. As Francis Ssennyonjo, our Uganda Partnership Manager, says, it is a tragic thing to see a man who is fully capable of feeding his family now confined in a camp relying on relief agencies to bring his family stale food. It is dehumanizing. It strips a person of self-respect.

As Francis quietly but firmly told me: "We want you to fight *with* us, not *for* us, in our war on poverty. No, we never want you to think you need to fight *for* us—that takes away our dignity. But, if you fight *with* us, and we understand each other at a deep level, then we can go a long way together."

Haiti

The Context

BY DOUG SEEBECK

I first met Mark Vanderwees in 1994, the year of the genocide in Rwanda. Mark and his wife, Nancy, were community development advisors in Haiti with the Christian Reformed World Relief Committee (CRWRC). When Haiti went through another one of its cycles of turmoil and political unrest, they and their young children were evacuated to Canada for three months. The timing was fortuitous, since we were looking for someone to do a rapid needs-assessment for the massive rehabilitation and reconciliation effort that was required in Rwanda after the massacre of nearly one million of its citizens.

Mark and I worked together in Rwanda for one month. We were able to put together a $1 million resettlement program in the Kitavu region near beautiful Lake Kivu. According to USAID, this program turned out to be one of their finest rehabilitation efforts. Lou Haveman, a friend in real estate (now a Partners Worldwide member) left his business for six months to come out and lead the entire volunteer effort. In the process, he developed a prototype for how our business partners could help change countries on a national scale.

When Haiti calmed down, Mark returned with his family. Neither of us knew at the time that those intense weeks in Rwanda would pave the way for an even more meaningful partnership in Haiti.

Four years later Mark attended Partners Worldwide's 1998 "Business as a Calling" conference in Chicago. He was deeply interested in helping some of his NGO partners in Haiti gain an income stream to pay for operational costs so they could focus their funding efforts on community projects. At the conference he had one question for a group of businesspeople who were interested in Haiti: "Would you come to personally evaluate the strategy we are deploying in Haiti, like that first team did in Kenya, and see how you can help?"

Milt Kuyers, Denny Hoekstra, and David Smies agreed to go. When the team arrived, they visited the office facilities of PWOFOD (Program for Training Diaconal Organizations), a Haitian NGO with whom CRWRC was collaborating. PWOFOD had managed to acquire land and a building, but it wanted to add a second story so they could rent it out to create a substantial revenue stream for their operations. The total cost of the project was approximately $40,000.

The entrepreneurs listened carefully and responded fairly quickly. "Partners Worldwide is in the business of creating jobs," they said, "and we're here to meet entrepreneurs who share that passion. But you have an interesting opportunity and a compelling vision, so we'll make you an offer. For every dollar you raise in Haiti within the next three months, we will provide you a 4-dollar match."

This was a completely novel proposal, and it wasn't met with great enthusiasm. No one in the NGO world had ever asked Haitians to put up anything—Haitians were perceived as recipients of charitable donations, not contributors. The leaders of PWOFOD left a bit deflated.

Nevertheless, they put the word out about this unusual matching offer, and within several months they had raised $8,000. Mark was stunned. The American partners had to scramble a little to put their $32,000 together. But it helped considerably when they told their friends that the Haitians had "skin in the game."

With the $40,000, the leaders of PWOFOD added a second floor to their facility. Then something unexpected happened again. When the Japanese embassy saw what PWOFOD had accomplished, they provided the resources needed to add a *third* floor. Today PWOFOD has filled both floors with tenants and is close to achieving its goal of organizational sustainability.

Much was learned through this entrepreneurial venture. CRWRC now provides matching grants to all its partners, the Haitian NGO discovered it had some healthy donors right in its own back yard, and the entrepreneurs in Haiti were excited by the ability to leverage their money.

Partners Worldwide also gained a great deal from this venture. Through the project Mark met three Haitian businesspeople who had contributed to PWOFOD's capital campaign: Ernso Jean-Louis, Ralph Edmond, and Sylvie Theard.

In 1999 I encouraged Mark to invite a team of Haitian businesspeople to Partners Worldwide's international conference. I asked him to bring at least half a dozen people if he could. Mark told me he knew of only three Christian businesspeople in the entire country: Ernso, Ralph, and Sylvie.

Those three friends did indeed come to the conference, and it proved to be a life-changing event for us all.

Maggie Steber

"Be a new breed of missionary that demonstrates the gospel by starting businesses that create jobs for the poor."

Ernso Jean-Louis

Bearing Much Fruit

BY TIMOTHY STONER

Ernso Jean-Louis is a rarity. He's a Haitian businessman who became successful as an "expat" and chose to return to help improve conditions in his desperately poor homeland.

Estimates indicate that around two million Haitians have fled the island to make a life in North America and Europe. There are no statistics tracking those like Ernso's family who have made the return trip home. Very few have had the courage or conviction to risk their comfort and safety for a possibility of helping others.

The first time I meet Ernso, it's February 2008 and he is speaking at Calvin College in Grand Rapids, Michigan, at a conference on faith and international development. He is both a businessman and a pastor, an explosive combination I have met in various parts of the world.

He begins by telling the story from John 15 in which Jesus, in his final strategic teaching before the crucifixion, is preparing his disciples for his death. They are walking together to the garden of Gethsemane, and Jesus is talking to them about plants, gardeners, and fruit bearing. It's a rural conversation among rural men who have grown up knowing the cycles of planting and harvesting. Jesus tells his friends, "I am the true vine and my Father is the gardener" (John 15:1). Jesus tells them that they are the "branches" that grow out of the main grapevine, and if they want to be productive they must remain connected to him because he is their source of nourishment and life.

So far Ernso hasn't said anything his audience hasn't heard before. But then he tells us that he's not there to speak about the gospel, but about sustainable business. He has my attention immediately—as well as the attention of several hundred college students in the room.

Ernso describes the abyss of poverty in his home country: 54% of the population live on one dollar a day, child mortality is three times higher than the worldwide average, and there are no accurate numbers to gauge the heartbreak of widespread unemployment. The barriers to growing a business in Haiti are almost impassible: lack of basic utilities and transportation, political and social instability, pervasive corruption on all levels, and rampant crime.

Ernso tells us that he believes his call and the call of others like him is to change Haiti not only with the gospel, but with business. He observes that missionaries have done a marvelous job of personal conversion (over 60% of the population claim to be Christian) but have had virtually no impact on society. Haiti, the country with the largest numbers of converts in the Western Hemisphere, is also one of the poorest countries.

I agree with Ernso's point. When conversion of millions makes no impact on a society, other than the construction of an inordinate number of church buildings, there is something very troubling going on.

Ernso tells us that he believes God is raising up a new breed of missionary who will proclaim the gospel *and* demonstrate the good news by starting businesses to provide jobs and eradicate poverty in the name of Jesus. He focuses on the exhortation of Jesus to "bear fruit that will remain." It is clear that, from his perspective, the impetus is Jesus, the power is from Jesus, and the goal is to introduce the poor to Jesus.

> Ernso tells us that he believes his call and the call of others like him is to change Haiti not only with the gospel, but with business.

The gospel, Ernso is convinced, is a means of healing—healing that must flow to every level of need: spiritual, physical, and material. He believes that the power of the cross can also be brought to bear on a nation's economic disease. Ernso's challenge to his listeners is straightforward: become one of the new breed of missionary that preaches the gospel among the poor using the vehicle of sustainable businesses to demonstrate that Jesus brings present and future hope; that eternal life begins here and now, and that Christ's message impacts life on earth, not just life in heaven.

Clearly, while providing work is not the end of the story, it is obvious to Ernso that if the story you tell the unemployed leaves them still starving and unemployed, you have not brought them very good news.

"We Can't Accept This!"

Four months later I am in Port-au-Prince, speaking with Ernso in a large warehouse that has been divided up into smaller rooms of varying sizes. It is the headquarters for Haiti Partners for Christian Development, the business incubator. One of the rooms is used by his wife, Gina, a chemist who manufactures personal care products. Another houses Yolene Chrisostome, a young entrepreneur who makes peanut butter and a Haitian beer; and another is home to Best Quality, a business that produces handbags, school satchels, and folders.

Ernso, one of 12 children, grew up in Jeremie, a small town on the southern end of the island, far from the capital. His father was a coffee farmer. Mr. Ismeo Jean-Louis helped all his children get a college education in the United States, though he had only a first-grade education himself.

If the story you tell the unemployed leaves them still starving and unemployed, you have not brought them very good news.

His life had a profound impact on Ernso. "The only book my father knew how to read or preach to us was the book of Proverbs. He was one of the wisest men I have ever known."

After high school Ernso was accepted at St. Augustine's College in Raleigh, North Carolina. A year later he moved to Chicago to study engineering at DeVry University. In 1984 he began working for Motorola as a systems engineer, while Gina was employed by Campbell Soup as a lab technician. They were content, successful, and were making good money. But their comfort was assaulted every time they heard news reports about Haitian boat people fleeing their country on flimsy crafts of all kinds to escape the poverty and instability of their homeland.

Ernso felt that God would not allow him to ignore the suffering of his countrymen. When the internal pressure became too great, Ernso told his wife in frustra-

Maggie Steber

They were content, successful, and were making good money. But their comfort was assaulted every time they heard news reports about Haitian boat people.

tion, "We can't accept this! Jobs need to be created for our people. It is not right to have all this and not go back and help." They consulted their fathers, both of whom had escaped Haiti. Their response was brief and to the point: "What are you *thinking* about? You're *crazy!*"

But in 1988, Ernso and Gina Jean-Louis decided that they had to return. Together they had reached the same conclusion: "We can do more in Haiti than we can do in the United States. We are needed there more than here." They concluded that their primary goal would be to make a difference in people's lives. And they would use a very specific focus: teaching young people to work. They would help the church and organizations, but their primary task would be starting businesses and training others to do the same.

Ernso's first job back in Haiti was with a company that provides electronic and computer services. He was earning 10% of what he was getting in the U.S. One of his responsibilities was providing tech support for computer systems. Then in 1991, while on a call at the office of a Texaco executive, he was presented with an unusual offer. Without any preliminaries or lengthy inquiries, the executive asked, "Do you want a gas station?"

Ernso's mouth dropped open. The offer was simple: Texaco would train him and he would become a third-party dealer. They would even throw in the gas to get started. So in 1992, after three weeks of training in Miami, Ernso opened up his Texaco station.

The timing was propitious. The U.S. had just imposed a trade embargo against Haiti after a military coup overthrew President Jean-Bertrand Aristide. The embargo was to remain in effect until Aristide was restored to power. Many nations followed suit, and the U.N. complied by imposed sanctions against Haiti. The impact was felt most painfully by the poor and by small businesses. But Ernso's gas station and Gina's small grocery store thrived. They had begun the store with six employees, and in less than three years they had three grocery stores with 55 employees.

Electrified by the Vision

During those years, Ernso believed that his calling was to start businesses, create jobs, and use a portion of his finances to help the needy. Then in 1999, Mark VanderWees, an employee of the Christian Reformed World Relief Committee, encouraged Ernso to attend a Partners Worldwide Conference in Grand Rapids.

Ernso agreed, and brought two business friends with him: Ralph Edmond and Sylvie Theard. Sylvie, the self-effacing member of the partnership owns Itala, the biggest pasta manufacturer in Haiti, which makes corn and wheat snacks as well as breads and pastries. Ralph is CEO of Farmatrix, a large pharmaceutical company.

John Perkins, the activist and author who founded the Christian Community Development Association and the John M. Perkins Foundation, was one of the speakers. It was during John's talk that Ernso heard for the first time a concept that would turn his perspective about business on its head. Using his experiences with the poor in the inner cities of the U.S. South, John illustrated how the good news of the gospel becomes real when the unemployed get jobs. He told how the hearts of the poor are opened up to the claims of Jesus when they are given hope as they tangibly experience the love of Jesus.

> He was electrified by the vision of business as a vocation every bit as significant in God's eyes as that of a missionary or a pastor.

From John Perkins, Ernso learned that business is not just a means of making a lot of money that can be used to do good things. He was electrified by the vision of business as a vocation every bit as significant as that of a missionary or a pastor.

The Incubator

God also used a brief discussion with Milt Kuyers about the opportunities for partnering in Haiti to plant an idea that would be the impetus for the three friends to form Haiti Partners for Christian Development (HPCD). The purpose of this "incubator" would be to mentor small businesses. Its long-term goal was to help eradicate poverty through job creation. Partners Worldwide helped by providing the model, giving advice, and making matching funds and business mentors available. Ernso wrote the bylaws, and HPCD was inaugurated in 2000.

HPCD gathered entrepreneurs into a large warehouse provided by Sylvie, where they would be provided utilities and security services at no cost. Partners Worldwide would provide mentors from the United States and matching funds to help small entrepreneurs. The goal was to "incubate" 10 businesses in five years with a minimum of five employees per business.

ENERSA, now a stable, medium-sized business, is an illustration of HPCD's effectiveness. Dependable electricity is a desperate need in Haiti. Blackouts are frequent, and in some places electricity is available only two or three hours per day. There are times where there is no power for weeks. Through Ernso and Ralph's mentoring help, ENERSA has become the first Haitian company to build solar-powered equipment. They manufacture solar street lights and traffic lights.

Now, as Ernso puts it, "Where darkness once reigned, light shines. Where there was chaos, order has come." Even at the gates of the Cité Soleil, one of the most notorious crime-infested shanty towns in the world, physical light has begun to break through the darkness. "Because of the location of the business incubator," he tells me, "most of ENERSA's employees are young men from Cité Soleil."

Despite these successes, in its first few years, HPCD experienced a string of failures. The entrepreneurs in the incubator had good ideas, but no experience. Rather than stimulating growth and initiative, the incubator worked in reverse by creating dependency. After five years, no business had "graduated" to self-sufficiency. The one great success was ENERSA, the company Ernso referred to in his speech at Calvin College, which grew from two to 14 employees and went off on its own.

These experiences led to a drastic change in HPCD's policies. Now an entrepreneur is required to attend a business program for six months before entering the incubator. The maximum length of stay is 12 months, and the business must grow to three employees during that time. If it succeeds, the business receives an incentive check as start-up capital to launch out on its own.

Attending Partners Worldwide's conference inspired Ernso to mentor others, but it also provided him with a mentor of his own. Partners connected him with Ron Kunnen, retired owner of Family Fare grocery stores, headquartered in Grand Rapids.

Though Ernso speaks of Ron with great respect and appreciation, their relationship had its challenges. Ernso explains that Ron sincerely wanted to help, but "it was very difficult for him since he could not understand Haitian culture." Ron found the culture shock and poverty overwhelming, so he and Ernso agreed to meet every four months in Miami instead. They were both committed to making their relationship work, and Ernso realized that a once-in-a-lifetime opportunity had been handed to him: "I was given a chance to work with a highly successful grocer with tremendous experience. I realized that if this did not work, I would be the loser."

Ron helped Ernso attend three grocers' conventions in Chicago. He also pushed Ernso to project into the future. Ernso's goal was to have at least four stores and a centralized warehouse. Ron lent Ernso half of the funds for its construction, and in 2002 the warehouse was completed. Ernso named it Kunnen Plaza in honor of his mentor. Their two-year formal mentoring relationship is now over, but it has mellowed and deepened into a rich friendship. And, although it was "hard work to overcome our cultural differences," Ernso says, "Ron has become like a father to me more than a mentor."

The Warehouse Church

After Ernso's warehouse was built, grocery prices fell dramatically and the cost of imports became exorbitant. Ernso could not fill the large warehouse, and could not rent it out due to the political turmoil surrounding Aristide's election. Out of desperation, Gina, Ernso, and their two children began going to the warehouse after church in the afternoon to pray. Friends started coming over to pray with them. Soon others joined the group.

During this economic downturn, Ernso had also been studying theology. He graduated in 2003 from Jacksonville Seminary in Port-au-Prince. When the prayer group at the warehouse had grown to 150 people, Ernso said, "It looks like God has given me a church to pastor." Partners Worldwide's impact is evident from the name he has given it: Independent Assembly of Christian Partners.

"Where they come from they see so many people die," he tells me. "The boys have to walk over dead bodies to get to school."

Five years later the church has several hundred members. What makes Ernso most happy, besides the fact that more than 100 people have been converted, is that several have started their own businesses. Ernso has helped 10 of his most gifted young people find sponsors to study in the United States. The pastor/ businessman looks at me and makes a request. It is something that concerns him greatly: "Pray that they will come back." Before leaving for college they all agreed to return after two years. I'm sure he told them the same thing he and Gina decided years earlier: "You are needed much more in Haiti than in North America."

On Sunday morning I attend an unforgettable church service at Ernso's warehouse. It begins with a call to worship sung in Creole by a male quartet. Two of the singers look like they are still in high school. The song is unfamiliar, but

Ernso (right) and the choir

it doesn't really matter. A mixed choir then takes their places, and strong music of praise and adoration cascades over me. When the choir launches into a full-throated chorus I feel like the joyful melody is bearing me away.

I have been in worship services on five continents, but I don't think any of them have matched the service at Ernso's church. I was stunned by the beauty, passion, and giftedness of the singers. They were so young, but they sang with such power and spiritual intensity.

After the service, Ernso tells me the story of the male quartet. They have named themselves "Sel"—the French word for "salt." They have had no formal training and they write their own songs. Their home is in Cité Soleil, where 300,000 people live in one of Haiti's poorest and most dangerous areas. It is a filthy, degrading, disease- and crime-infested shanty town, considered one of the biggest slums in the Northern Hemisphere. There are few police, no sewers, no stores, no electricity. Armed gangs roam about spreading terror and death.

Pastor Ernso has encouraged the members of Sel to pray and sing for sick people in the hospital. They have gone into the poorest areas of the city and into the homes of the very wealthy to perform private concerts and to pray. Ernso is providing school fees as well as paying the costs of producing their first CD. "Where they come from they see so many people die," he tells me. "The boys have to walk over dead bodies to get to school."

But Samuel, Tassy, Apha, and Joseph are able to look beyond what their eyes see all around them. They are writing and singing songs about restoration. Two brothers and two friends with no fathers, living in one of the worst slums in the world, are being salt and light and are giving testimony to the transforming power of God. And they are doing so with music whose beauty can melt the hardest heart, for it points away from death to life, from despair to hope.

Bearing Much Fruit

At the end of his talk at Calvin College, Pastor Ernso Jean-Louis points us back to John 15. Jesus is about to leave the earth and his disciples are about to feel the disorienting pain of apparent failure and abandonment. Ernso quotes what is both a troubling warning and an encouraging promise: "I am the true vine, and my Father is the gardener. He cuts off every branch in me that bears no fruit, while every branch that does bear fruit he prunes so that it will be even more fruitful" (John 15:1-2).

> Two brothers and two friends with no fathers, living in one of the worst slums in the world, are being salt and light and are giving testimony to the transforming power of God.

In the context of business, he implies, a truly "fruitful" entrepreneur not only starts his own business, he multiplies his effectiveness by helping others do so. In an entrepreneurial context, fruitful Christians are those who impart their business skills to others who can create enterprises that provide the blessing of employment. And they do so through the love, ability, and energy Christ gives them to display the Father's compassion for the poor and the needy.

Business majors and international development students leave the chapel with an impassioned exhortation ringing in their ears: be one of the new breed of missionary that bears much (business) fruit, so the poor may taste and see that God is gracious and merciful and cares about their bodies as well as their souls.

But as Ernso, the pastor/businessman, reminds us all, it is only possible to bear life-giving, physically and spiritually sustaining fruit if we remain in the Vine, for as Jesus said, "Apart from me you can do nothing" (John 15:5). And we have his word on it that if we do remain in him and give our lives away by serving the poor, whatever our vocation, our Father in heaven will be glorified.

And that is the best long-term business incentive one could ever want.

Maggie Steber

"How can I help you?"

Ralph Edmond

Community Builder

BY TIMOTHY STONER

I n the heart of Port-au-Prince, the capital of Haiti, is a rarity: a successful and growing manufacturing company. Farmatrix employs 82 people and last year grossed over $2 million. In a country whose per capita income is about two dollars per day, this is a high-flying business.

I am in the office of Ralph Edmond, Farmatrix's CEO. He has a boyish face, but an intensity sparks from him. My first thought is "politics." He has the handsome face, the intelligence, the charisma, and an internal engine that seems to run most comfortably in fifth gear.

Ralph looks like he would fit in on Wall Street or in London, The Hague, Madrid, or any other metropolitan center that runs on and churns out money. But that is not where he lives, nor where he grew up. Ralph's boyhood town was the capital of one of the poorest countries in the Western Hemisphere. And here he remains—by choice, I will find out, and at a real cost. His story is not one of rags to riches, but temporary riches to lasting treasure.

Doing What *Should* Be Done

Ralph was born in 1961 into privilege. He studied at St. Louis de Gonzague, an elite parochial school. His father was an accountant; his mother, Mme Solange Vieux Edmond, was an anesthesiologist. It would seem the business drive came from her side. During Ralph's childhood years, Mme Edmond began importing pharmaceutical products and opened several drug stores. After high school, Ralph chose to walk through the doors she had opened and attended pharmacy school in Haiti. After graduation he then traveled to the U.S. to further his studies with an emphasis in business, majoring in marketing and finance at Baruch College in New York. He graduated magna cum laude.

In 1989, Ralph and his best friend, Alain Vincent, whose dad owned pharmacies in Haiti, decided to start Farmatrix. Their plan was to manufacture pharmaceuticals rather than importing them. These would be products with a "Haitian flair."

When they started, Ralph and Alain had the equivalent of $2,000 in funds and three employees. Every step in the manufacturing process was done by hand. Their company had a simple and very limited product line: a soothing ointment similar to Ben-Gay, a douche, and an antiseptic for hospitals. They diversified quickly into syrups, antacids, and multivitamins. They are now entering a new niche market of herbal energy drinks. Their marketing byline is *"Men fos la"* — "Here is your strength!" Their newest venture is perfume with a unique and distinctly Haitian provenance and their market is the huge Haitian "diaspora"— those expats (many quite successful) who fled Haiti for the more hospitable shores of North America and Europe. From three products, Farmatrix has now upwards of 45.

Ralph and Alain looked carefully at the business environment of their country and took special note of things that didn't work. What they concluded was that being underhanded and deceptive, paying bribes, and breaking the law was not working all that well. They decided that they were going to try something else: "doing what *should* be done," as Ralph says. So, at the top of their list for a new way of doing business in Haiti was respecting the laws of the land. They made an inflexible commitment to "be responsible to the government and to our brothers." Specifically, this meant that, unlike most companies in Haiti, they would pay all taxes owed, plus they would commit to be involved in their community.

Ralph smiles broadly. "The mindset of the business elite is like that of Robin Hood. They justify robbing the government of taxes by arguing that the money is going to help entrepreneurs create jobs, increase national wealth, and become fiscally responsible." Of course it does no harm to Robin Hood's bottom line either. "They would always ask us, 'Why should I pay taxes to a government of thieves?'" Ralph would answer back, "But who is stealing first, the government who misuses the money, or the business owner who keeps the money?" Apparently there was no counter-argument, but I get the impression Ralph failed to convince very many of his peers.

A Platform to Connect

In late 1999, Ralph, Ernso Jean-Louis, and Sylvie Theard established Haiti Partners for Christian Development, a branch of Partners Worldwide. What attracted Ralph was the commitment to bridging the gap between the rich and poor. "In Haiti, these groups never meet," he says. "HPCD created a platform for rich and poor to connect by placing all of us on the same level. We were all primarily entrepreneurs, whether rich or poor."

But Ralph had not always been so favorably disposed to this North American NGO. Mark Vanderwees, director of community development with CRWRC, had been inviting Ralph to come to the United States for one of their international conferences. Ralph kept politely declining. He was, frankly, suspicious. As a Catholic he had a healthy skepticism of the motive behind this Protestant man's invitations. He was pretty certain that evangelicals were using business conferences primarily as a ploy to convert non-Protestants. Finally, in June 1999, he gave in. He traveled with Ernso and Sylvie to Calvin College in Grand Rapids, Michigan, where the meetings were held.

"HPCD created a platform for rich and poor to connect by placing all of us on the same level. We were all primarily entrepreneurs, whether rich or poor."

After the first few sessions, Milt Kuyers came up to the three Haitians, who were sitting at a round table having refreshments, and asked them a question. By American standards it was not earth-shattering, but it almost floored Ralph. The look on his face tells me that it still amazes him. After introducing himself, Milt bent down to look directly at the three business owners and asked, "How can I help you?" Ralph looked over at Ernso, his eyebrows raised with the unspoken question: "Okay, what's up with the white guy? What's the catch?"

Ralph turns toward me, a very serious look on his face now. "Tim, nobody had ever asked me that question in Haiti. I was immediately very skeptical. I am used to a culture where if you want to do something for me, there must be something you want to get from me in return." Milt sat down with the three friends and began asking if there were other business owners in Haiti that were like them. "He wanted to know if we knew of others whom we could invite to start a chapter of Partners Worldwide in Haiti. That got us thinking about what we could do in our country."

Later, when Ralph was in the home of another board member, Dave Smies, who had been to Haiti just nine months earlier, something made an even more profound impact on him. Over coffee one evening, Ralph and Dave were discussing stewardship. Somewhat offhandedly, Dave mentioned that he and his wife, Deb, had decided to give 50% of their earnings to God. Ralph was almost speechless. "Could you please repeat that?" he asked, after regaining his composure.

Dave repeated the statement. Ralph's follow-up question was obvious: "Why?"

"Because everything I have belongs to God," was the startling reply. Ralph's worldview was undergoing a Copernican revolution. "I was shocked!" he tells me, understating his astonishment. He could not comprehend this mentality; his first thought was, "This is really weird!"

"When you build something in Haiti, it can be at the cost of your life. You put your own and your family's life at risk." He spreads out his hands, just telling me the

> **"When you build something in Haiti, it can be at the cost of your life. In my country, business is a dangerous vocation."**

facts. "In my country, business [making money] is a dangerous vocation."

Ralph is not exaggerating; death has come very close. "We have been victimized on several occasions. Going to work once, while stopped at a busy intersection, a guy with a 9-mm gun ran toward my car and began firing. I was driving, four bullets went into the car, one almost hit me in my spine, and my chauffeur who happened to be sitting on the passenger side was shot and almost killed." Several of his peers and family members have been kidnapped and released only after paying a hefty ransom.

"So when we build a successful business, we automatically conclude, 'This money belongs to me! I risked my life for it, and if you want it, you will have to take it from me by force!'" Ralph clenches his fists but grins at me behind his silver and black frames as he illustrates this very logical possessiveness.

Another impediment to generosity in Haiti is that there is little incentive for charitable giving. North Americans are guaranteed a tax deduction to sweeten the pill, but in Haiti this is not the case. Many charitable organizations run on an informal basis. As a result, a tax deduction may or may not be forthcoming, depending upon several discretionary factors, such as whether the treasury department concludes your financial records are in order and you have been "faithful" in paying taxes.

Though Ralph admits he initially thought Dave and Deb's commitment to stewardship was "weird," their conversation made him re-evaluate his nominal Christianity. Not long after returning to Haiti, he decided to take his faith seriously and became a committed follower of Jesus.

Ralph tells me that before he attended the Partners Worldwide conference, his relationship to God was such that "God was not present in my everyday life. Life was very compartmentalized. God was in church on Sunday, and he was *only* present in church. He was not in my business." He shakes his head at how his understanding has changed. "Before the Partners conference, my understanding was that God and my daily life were separated. God had nothing to do with my business."

Milt's straightforward question had also struck home. It had so impacted Ralph, Ernso, and Sylvie that they returned to Port-au-Prince with one burning question: What can we do to help the poor in Haiti? That question provided the impetus to form Haiti Partners for Christian Development (HPCD).

"It was our way of asking Haiti, 'How can I help you?'" They began asking other Haitians in business the same question Milt had asked them. At the heart was the revolutionary realization that their vocation as businesspeople was from God and that God wanted them to use their skills, their time, and their wealth to bless others as they themselves had been blessed.

Service to Others

Ralph is a born mentor, I soon discover. Despite surface appearances, what drives him as much as the success of his company is the opportunity to help others learn how to become successful in business and in life. Besides mentoring entrepreneurs and small business owners, Ralph has been led to expand his service to others.

Two years ago he felt God directing him to invest a significant amount of time in St. Martin, a community that lies adjacent to his pharmaceutical plant and is one of the most violent areas of Port-au-Prince. Working along with Concern, an Irish NGO with long and painful experience in conflict resolution, he promotes dialogue between gang members, businesspeople, and political leaders in the community. "All sectors of St. Martin are

> Ralph defines mentoring as "two people sharing their lives."

beginning to talk to each other. The first year all I did was spend time building relationships. I was just developing trust. We are now in the development stage where we have formed a committee representing all segments of society to discuss how we can build into the community, not against it."

What Ralph found compelling was the opportunity to work alongside businesspeople whose goal was to improve the community by helping others. He was convinced that this would help alleviate some of the social tensions that he believes "are the basis for much of the violence in my country." HPCD gave him a platform to fulfill his deepest passion.

As we talk, Ralph is getting more animated and his face is lighting up. "Through our organization we can share our knowledge with the smaller guys and then share our own lives." This successful CEO is letting me in on what makes him tick. It is not the subtle power of speaking down to people, or the quiet glory of dazzling the less gifted or educated with a superior skill set or knowledge base. Ralph defines mentoring as "two people sharing their lives." What he most enjoys is personal engagement, investing his life in the lives of others, not just dispensing information or taking his company to the next level.

On average, he spends six hours a week in this social development work. "It is not something separate from my business. It is all part of what God has called me to do." He stops to underline the seriousness of his conviction. "It *is* my work." I don't think I've ever heard a CEO in North America explain his service to others in those terms. One simple question born out of genuine interest and compassion nine years earlier has taken Ralph farther than most of his peers.

The St. Martin committee is planning a major project to manufacture charcoal from waste. Ralph is also involved with the Haitian Tennis Federation, overseeing their junior program. It is the latter that Ralph believes will be the most effective

for giving those below the age of 18 (50% of Haiti's population) a reason not to get involved with gangs.

Letting God Be Involved

What has transformed the thinking of this progressive and driven CEO is the realization that "you can do business by letting God be involved." I ask him how this has impacted his life. He answers immediately, but his answer is unexpected: "It has changed how I worship God." He now meets once a week with a core group of "business guys" who hold each other accountable. Ralph has learned not only to do his work for God and to depend upon him, but to depend on his brothers as well. "We ask each other the hard questions." It's obvious that this group is very important in Ralph's life. Though he speaks with a smile, there is a steely glint in his eyes as he expands: "We pursue those who are not going the right way." I gather that, for this group of men, accountability is not just a nice Christian slogan. "They had to pursue me last year," he admits. "I was going the wrong way." He does not elaborate and I do not press him. Whatever the problem was, it's clear Ralph's peers helped him climb back on the narrow road.

"Letting God be involved" has also changed how Ralph runs his business. Beyond providing a fair wage to his employees, he has chosen something even more unusual for a country steeped in mystery, shadow, and under-the-table payments. He has embraced a philosophy of transparency. There are no secrets. Those with a genuine need to know can get all the financial information they request, and it will be complete and accurate.

Besides being treated fairly, Ralph's employees receive a benefit few enjoy on the island: health insurance. They also receive on-the-job professional development opportunities. "We get them involved in managing the business. We are working on decentralization; delegating responsibility. We are teaching them responsibility and accountability," says Ralph. Farmatrix is clearly a corporation that is setting the national standard for how to run your business right.

Part of the Solution

Our conversation turns to the broader social climate in Haiti. "It is very hard to keep hope alive here," Ralph says. "It is so much easier to leave and work in the United States." He illustrates the point. "Two years ago, my sister and sister-in-law were kidnapped in separate incidents. After their families paid the ransom, both families decided to leave for Miami." I find out later that Ralph left part of the story out. Ted and Jan Boers, who are investing heavily in Haiti's economic development, give me the rest of the story.

Ralph's sister was abducted, that is true. What he failed to explain was that as soon as he found this out, he went directly to his mother's house and pulled out all the phones. Mme Solange Vieux Edmond was struggling with severe depression, and Ralph believed that the emotional pressure of dealing with the kidnappers could harm her irreparably. Being attuned to high-level negotiations, he also feared that if the kidnappers sensed weakness on the other end of the line, they might keep his sister indefinitely as they ratcheted up their demands. So Ralph forced the kidnappers to negotiate personally with him. Eventually the ransom was paid and his sister was released.

"So what keeps you going? What keeps you here?" I ask him. He looks around at his spartan conference room and at the product displays on the wall. "I am building things. I am building a company. I have hope." He did almost decide to bail out on Haiti, he admits. The kidnapping of his sister and the shooting incident a month later that almost killed his driver were the last straw. He decided in 2006 to send his family to live in Texas. "But after a few months my wife, Chantal (who used to be the administrative officer of the Peace Corps in Haiti), said we all had to leave or we all were going to stay. Separation was not an option. 'We are going to be together,' she said, 'but if we stay we have to stay differently. We have to stay for a reason bigger than just because of business.'"

Ralph explains why he chose not to remove his corporation to safer, more hospitable environs. "I don't want to run from the problem—I want to be part of resolving it. Even though I may have only 10 businesspeople who will stand with me, we will stand together as part of the solution for Haiti." He is not trying to impress me with boastful talk. I am hearing a brave man explain honestly what is motivating his conduct. Then he gives me another glimpse into the spiritual dimension behind his choice not to turn his back on Haiti. "The solu-

"Even though I may have only 10 businesspeople who will stand with me, we will stand together as part of the solution for Haiti."

tion to the problems in Haiti will be through fiscally and socially responsible people who understand the work of God in their lives."

He used to be driven by a need to change the nation, he tells me. Now he does not give it as much thought. "I'm not worried about whether Haiti is going to be changed. Now what I realize is that if what I am doing changes others, *I* will be changed. Whether Haiti is changed is God's issue."

At the moment there are at least three others on his side. They are the members of his core group. Daniel Rouzier owns car dealerships: Honda, Hyundai, and GM. Louis Mars, a former business owner, is now involved full time in dialogue for national reconciliation. Kenneth Michel imports rice and sugar. "The four of us are staying in Haiti for a reason: to do it differently. We may have to leave, but we don't worry about it. We are committed to building relationships." Their work, in St. Martin particularly, has evidently produced dividends. "When gang members invite you to come to an event in the middle of gang-warfare land, you know you are doing something right."

Building a Community

Although Ralph assures me that he has placed Haiti's future in God's hands, he has not shut his eyes to her desperate plight. He is running his business as a model for others to emulate. He is investing his life in individual and community transformation, and he wants God to keep changing him. But the fate of his nation still weighs heavily on him.

"We must see ourselves as one country. We have no choice but to live together." He has thought this all through very carefully, and he is about to say something that is a variation of a theme I have heard on several continents. It runs counter to the philosophy that has driven decades of compassionate giving. "We can't depend on something coming from abroad. All the outside help has not improved the country."

But Ralph is about to branch off into new territory I have not heard before. "Haiti is a community of people. The base of that community is families. We have to start at the family level. If we build strong families we can build a strong nation. The care you put into building your family is what you will do to build your country." As he talks I can't help but think that I may be hearing the foundational planks of a national campaign. As an aside Ralph explains how many national leaders have mistresses. It's an accepted way of life. "I tell them, 'Forget your political plans and go back to your wife and children. *Then* come back and lead

"If we build strong families we can build a strong nation. The care you put into building your family is what you will do to build your country."

the country. Look after your family and *then* take care of the community."' Is this guy electable? I wonder again.

Of course I need to know how he builds a solid family in this hostile environment. Before arriving at Farmatrix, Lesly Jules, Partners Worldwide's in-country partnership manager, gave me a clue. "I never call him on Saturday," he tells me. "Saturday is family day."

"Good for him," I say. I'm glad to hear that this type-A guy is keeping his eye on the right ball. Ralph, being who he is, has learned to multitask, though. His boys are a part of the junior tennis program he oversees for the National Sports Federation. So when he is supporting the federation at competitions, he is supporting his sons at the same time.

I ask him about political aspirations. His answer is impressive. "Business *is* my politics. I want to be part of a new model for community transformation. I think that in St. Martin I am having a greater impact than I would have were I to become a politician. If I build my family and one community, who knows what broader impact that might have?"

He returns to his love for mentoring. "At HPCD we choose young entrepreneurs, and it is through them that we are engaged in community building." Through this organization scores have been helped. The question Milt asked Ralph several years earlier is now being asked of hundreds of Haitians, and it is producing a harvest of blessing. What Ralph has recognized is that by asking "How can I help you?" he is offering not finances or strategies, but his own life. "My interest is the time we spend sharing our lives, so that we can build a community together. Then if that community becomes a healthy and strong country, that is up to God."

May it be so.

Haiti: Reflections *by Doug Seebeck*

In 1999 Partners Worldwide held its third annual conference, titled "Business '99: An Outstanding Christian Calling." Bill Pollard, CEO of ServiceMaster, gave a powerful keynote address about becoming a values-driven business. It was a memorable talk, but for Ralph Edmond there were two very different things that made a profound impact on him: the time he spent in Dave Smies's home, and those five simple words from Milt Kuyers: "How can I help you?"

At the end of the conference, Milt introduced me to Ralph Edmond, Ernso Jean-Louis, and Sylvie Theard. The trio expressed their desire to start an organization called Haitian Partners for Christian Development (HPCD). At the time our name was "Partners for Christian Development," and this was the first time an international business affiliate wanted to adopt our name in their country.

I told the three that they had our blessing as long as they were in agreement with some foundational commitments "Taking our name means that you buy into our vision for business as ministry for a world without poverty, you believe our core values, and you will commit to measuring the number of businesses you are growing and how many jobs you create and sustain each year. If you are okay with that, we'll do whatever we can to help you grow the movement in Haiti."

They made a promise in return. "Give us three months. We will register a legal entity with a constitution and bylaws and will have written plans for formally launching this in January 2000. We'll also show you the businesses we have helped." They were true to their word, and at their invitation, exactly three months later, I was on a plane to Haiti to see what they had accomplished. I was astonished by their progress. They had met or surpassed all their goals and had experienced one major success with a micro-entrepreneur named Hugo Philemy.

Hugo is creative, innovative, tireless, and can do a lot with limited resources. His family raised bees that produced a significant amount of honey, so Hugo decided to start a honey business with a micro-loan from PWOFOD—the same organization the Partners team had helped in their first venture.

Because Hugo couldn't afford to buy bottles for packaging, he came up with an innovative solution. He found empty Heinz catsup bottles in one of the many dumps in Port-au-Prince. He cleaned the bottles; created his own black-and-white label; filled the bottles with home-grown Haitian honey, and sealed them with tin foil. The dark, beautiful honey was delicious, but the makeshift packaging prevented Hugo from selling his product commercially, so he sold it in small quantities on the streets.

Ernso Jean-Louis and Ralph Edmond knew Hugo because they were donors of PWOFOD. Together they came up with a plan. On the shelves of Ernso's chain of Red Star supermarkets were bottles of honey imported from the United States. Hugo's honey was better, and it was local. So Ralph arranged for the company that packaged all his liquid pharmaceuticals to bottle Hugo's honey as well. Randy Vander Ploeg of ShipPac in Kalamazoo, Michigan, offered marketing assistance and encouraged Hugo to provide nutritional information on the label.

Maggie Steber

The Lefèvres with popsicle distributors and employees

I vividly recall the excitement when these founders of HPCD showed me what they had done. Hugo's product was transformed. It was in a presentable plastic bottle, was heat-sealed, and sported a colorful picture on the front and a nutritional label on the back. It looked just as good as the imported honey, but its price was significantly lower than that of the U.S. brand, with better taste, quality, and provenance. Ralph calculated that he had invested 30 hours and $1,500 over 60 days. Hugo's business grew so fast he went from being self-employed to an employer of eight. But, like so many Haitians before him, his success increased his personal risk, and he decided to take his business skills to the more hospitable business climate of Canada.

Haitian Partners for Christian Development was officially launched in January 2000. Sylvie and her husband, Stanley, provided space in their facility for HPCD to operate. Today, the organization includes about 50 Christian business and professional people in Port-au-Prince who are committed to supporting each other and developing Christian business groups in cities all over Haiti. HPCD has also established a business incubator in Port-au-Prince, where small businesses can grow while they share the costs of electricity, water, security and office equipment.

Another entrepreneur in the HPCD network who has been significantly helped by Partners Worldwide is Marie Michelle Lefèvre Africo ("Madame Lefèvre"). She taught French in secondary schools, but her Catholic beliefs prodded her to do something concrete to help the poor in her community. So about 10 years ago she began a small popsicle business. She began with one freezer and sold out of her house. Today, as a result of a series of loans from PWOFOD and mentoring help from the Partners Worldwide network, she operates a business with 22 freezers, 40 employees in the factory, and 500 independent business operators. Her rainbow-colored ices are sold throughout Port-au-Prince. Madame Lefèvre is an incredible success story.

And fortunately for Haiti, she has no intention of going anywhere more comfortable. She wants to be the leading popsicle business in Haiti. "God is the provider, and I will not rest until I supply jobs to all families in Haiti," she says.

In addition to her strong faith, Madame is motivated by the success of her employees and distributors. They earn, on average, double what their peers earn in the marketplace. Those earnings have been invested in building new homes, in quality education for their children (in come cases at the university level), in improved health care, and in these employees venturing out to start their own enterprises as a result of the training, encouragement, and mentoring she so willingly provides.

Hugo and Madame Lefèvre are perfect examples of the economic challenges faced by the developing world's entrepreneurs, and why successful people like Ernso, Ralph, and Sylvie are absolutely vital to Haiti's future. It's also a testimony to the need for organizations like PWOFOD and HPCD.

As you have seen, Ernso, Ralph, and Sylvie contributed to significantly growing Partners Worldwide's work in Haiti. Ted Boers, from our hometown of Grand Rapids, also helped shape our organization in significant ways.

Ted founded Datacomp, which specializes in appraising manufactured housing. Ted was entering his early 50s when he read *Halftime* by Bob Buford. The book brought him up short. It prompted him to ask God: "What is it that you want me to do with the second half of my life?"

For no particular reason that Ted can identify, he became interested in Haiti. As the small country began to loom large in Ted's thoughts, his college-age daughter Kristen was getting ready to spend a month there. Ted asked her to look around for something a "business guy like me" could do in a country like that. She came back with contact information for Partners Worldwide. After his first trip in 2002, his initial feelings were only confirmed. "I was totally affirmed. I felt like I was home," he says.

During his report in our monthly teleconference call with our U.S. partners, where we share best practices, Ted issued a challenge. "I really don't know how much good I did," he admitted. "If I am going to be a mentor, spending my time and my dollars going to Haiti, then I probably need a few more tools in my toolbox from Partners Worldwide. That way I won't feel like I'm shooting in the dark."

Those words inspired our Million Mentors Initiative, a four-year program that we implemented in Haiti, Nicaragua, and Kenya in conjunction with USAID's Global Development Alliance. Its purpose was to help streamline our business model, perfect the partnership process, develop a training program for mentors, and provide better resources for the entrepreneurs in their partnerships. Our end goal was to evaluate the effectiveness of these business-to-business partnerships to test whether our model was indeed worthy of a larger scale.

A team of outside economists, led by Dr. Roland Hoksbergen of Calvin College, did an extensive evaluation of our efforts in 2007. Their findings were encouraging. The goals for the initiative were exceeded: 84 business associations/cooperatives and 4,516 business members had created and sustained 5,063 jobs. Based on 365 quantitative, independent surveys of participating business owners, the evaluators found that:

- 65% had higher profits.
- 71% had higher incomes.
- 76% reported the value of their businesses had increased.
- 87% attributed their success to their participation in the business affiliate.

The success wasn't limited to the business owners. Over 200 employees participated in the study completed by the independent survey teams, and these results were also encouraging:

- 70% of the employees' families improved their economic well-being.
- 76% developed marketable skills through their jobs.
- 85% like their job.
- 89% said they were treated well or very well at work.
- 90% said their job was important or very important to their family's well-being.

The survey also showed that people's lives were being transformed:

- 68% were mentoring others for the first time, because of their affiliation with Partners Worldwide.
- 71% had increased their charitable giving.
- 72% had increased the amount of time they are volunteering in their community.
- 77% reported applying more ethical business practices.
- 84% were more satisfied in being a business owner, largely because of their new understanding of business as a calling.
- 81% said mentoring was the significant factor influencing these changes.

The evaluators' final report said, "Over and over again we heard about the importance of the overall vision that emphasized business as calling, business as mission and values such as responsible stewardship and community service."

The Haitian partners are praying for nothing less than a transformed nation, and that is what Ted and Jan are devoting the rest of their lives to. Jesus said, "Truly I tell you, if you have the faith of a mustard seed, you can tell that mountain to move into the sea, and it will." Mountains of corruption, unjust structures, dysfunctional relationships, and greed: all these mountains will go. In Haiti, they are already beginning to crumble.

Manila

PHILIPPINES

Malaysia

Brunei

Indonesia

The Philippines

The Context

BY DOUG SEEBECK

While planning for this book we had to make some strategic decisions about which countries we would cover, and—what was more difficult—which we would leave out. I wanted to include a chapter on the Philippines, but as the stack of manuscript pages began looking like the Leaning Tower of Pisa, we decided we simply could not fit it in.

About that time I was introduced to Larry Ross, a well-known figure in Christian media and marketing who has worked with people like Billy Graham and Rick Warren. Larry cut to the heart. "Have you gone with Tim on any of his interview trips?" he asked. I had not, since I had wanted to avoid influencing what Tim learned. Larry was polite, but he proceeded to let me know that if I wanted to maximize the impact of this project for Partners Worldwide, I had better become more involved. For me, that reinforced the rationale of including the Philippines, but our staff wasn't so sure. The budget was tight. Time was short.

Then we had our annual partnership summit for the North American team leaders. At that summit, Paul Holwerda and Elaine Hoekstra, co-leaders for our North American Philippines affiliate, presented a case study on what can go wrong in a partnership. It was a sobering talk, and it was evident they were hurting. Paul had been involved from the beginning of the formation of e-BEST (Evangelical Businesspeople and Entrepreneurs for Social Transformation), our affiliate in the Philippines. Just a few years earlier e-BEST had been a flourishing organization with hundreds of members, but what they shared with us was a story of struggle, disappointment, and, apparently, a total organizational meltdown.

After that meeting Tim approached me with an observation. "In all my travels and in all my interviews, I haven't really heard anything that would suggest there are any serious difficulties in these partnerships. For the most part all I'm hearing is good news." He looked at me pointedly. "You said that we wanted to have a realistic picture. We know that it isn't all success. We know how painful the partnership journey can be, and we want those who get involved to have a realistic perspective. From what Paul and Elaine said, I think we should share the lessons learned not only from victory, but from defeat."

Within that same week an email arrived from Dr. Tito Contado, the president of e-BEST. The subject line was in bold capital letters that read "TIRED AND DISCOURAGED IN THE PHILIPPINES." It was a report from a committed and persevering partner who had been through a long battle and was losing heart.

At Partners Worldwide we often say that we want to follow where the Spirit is leading. We routinely pray, "Lord, shut firmly the doors we are not supposed to go through, and open those that we are not aware of." As I thought over the email and what Tim had said, I began to feel that this was a door God was beckoning us through. I told the team, "We're going to the Philippines. This partnership and the people in it need our encouragement and support." After a brief discussion they agreed.

Tim and I had been in Manila for less than 24 hours when it became obvious that it had been God issuing the invitation to come. We had been summoned to be agents of reconciliation but to also receive great encouragement in the process.

"Success is measured by how much you've helped others."

Tito Contado

Agriculturalist to Entrepreneur

BY TIMOTHY STONER

en years ago, at age 62, Dr. Tito Contado left the United Nations Food and Agriculture Organization (FAO) in Rome with a healthy pension and retirement package. He had worked there for 20 years, and, as they say, he was set for life. "I told him he could just enjoy his retirement and write all the books he wanted," says his wife, Lou, with a smile.

It was tempting, but for Tito that was not enough. He and Lou decided to leave their comfortable existence in Italy, return to their homeland in the Philippines, and begin a new phase of life driven by a passion for serving others as entrepreneurs. That decision changed their perspective on economic and social development and gave them a renewed sense of calling in the world.

Doug Seebeck and I visited the Contados at their spacious home in Los Baños, about an hour and a half south of Manila. As they told us their story, we once again saw the hand of God.

Leading Them Home

Tito Contado was born in 1936 in Eastern Samar—one of the most remote areas of the Philippines. Both his parents were schoolteachers. When Tito was 13, his mother died of tuberculosis. Just one year later, his father passed away due to infection from appendicitis. Tito and his five siblings, now orphans, went to live with their aunt and uncle.

At age 15 Tito enrolled in a national agricultural school in western Leyte as a "working student." That meant that he went to school in the mornings and in the afternoons he worked on the school farm. Tito graduated at the top of the class of 1956. He told several of his friends who were interested in church ministry, "You can become pastors and I will be a rich farmer and support you."

After one year of farming he decided to further his education in an agricultural educational program at Visayas Agricultural College. Tito lived with Lou's older sister and her husband, who ran a boarding house. To pay for room and board, Tito cut firewood, took care of the garden, raised the pigs, and did maintenance work.

He graduated cum laude in 1960 and became a teacher of vocational agriculture at his alma mater. After teaching for a year he married Loida (Lou) Badrina Managbanag, who had just finished a degree in theology from Silliman University.

The following year Tito was awarded a graduate fellowship by the University of the Philippines to pursue a master's degree in agricultural education and animal science. With degree in hand he accepted a job offer from the university's College of Agriculture. The Rockefeller Foundation later awarded him a scholarship to pursue Ph.D. studies at Cornell University, which he completed in 1968.

After 12 years of teaching and serving as the Director of Extension of the College of Agriculture, Tito was approached by the United Nations Food and Agriculture Organization and offered a position at their world headquarters in Rome. He accepted, and in 1978 Tito and Lou and their three children left the Philippines for Italy.

It was a good life, and Tito eventually became the Chief of the Service. But as retirement drew near, Tito and Lou sensed God leading them to return home to start businesses and help encourage other Filipino entrepreneurs to become successful to create wealth and provide jobs for the poor.

"God's Gift to Mankind"

With the money from their retirement package, Tito and Lou purchased a large house with a basement that would sleep 30 people and opened a guest house. When they learned that a friend's gas station was failing, they purchased half of the equity and agreed to co-manage the business. Though it was a good start, they knew they were called to do more.

Tito began researching new agricultural breakthroughs that could be successfully commercialized. Through Lou's sister he was introduced to a tropical medicinal plant scientifically known as *morinda citrofolia*. This plant's medicinal qualities had been documented several years earlier by two North Americans vacationing in Tahiti. During their visit they were struck by the remarkable and uniform health and longevity of the local villagers. After making inquiries, they discovered the secret: a bulbous fruit from a small leafy tropical tree growing along the island shore. The fruit is known affectionately as *Noni*, but Tito refers to it as "God's gift to mankind."

Thorough scientific study revealed that this unassuming little plant "has more nutraceuticals than any other known fruit on the planet," as Tito says. Noni's devotees use its dark, sour liquid extract for everything from healing cuts and acne to treating diabetes. Lou gestures at her white hair. "When I returned from Rome, it was thinning out very much," she admits. Now she has a full head of beautiful hair. "Noni regenerates cells that are dying," Dr. Tito explains. He has been using it daily for years. His cardiologist was so impressed by his quick recovery from bypass surgery on six of his arteries that she began taking Noni. I can't deny that the Contados look and act 10 years younger than their real ages.

> The fruit is known affectionately as Noni, but Dr. Tito refers to it as "God's gift to mankind."

To produce and market this potent food supplement, Tito established Philippine Morinda Citrifolia, Inc. It employs 15 workers, 40 marketers, and 20 collectors who gather the fruit from the island shores. Their marketing representative is Rowell Manza, an orphan whom Tito and Lou helped put through school. At present they are producing more than 600 liters of Noni extract a month, and they are building a facility that may quadruple that output.

Once again, life was good for the Contados. But a difficult challenge was in store.

e-BEST Begins

In 2001 Tito was approached by CRWRC staff to help establish an organization called e-BEST (Evangelical Businesspeople and Entrepreneurs for Social Transformation). It was to be an international affiliate of Partners Worldwide whose mission was to provide Christian fellowship, mentoring relationships, and access to capital for small businesses. In September 2002, e-BEST was registered with the Securities and Exchange Commission as a nonprofit corporation.

"Our foundational commitment was to impact community change," Dr. Tito explains. "Microfinance at the poverty line must be connected with the wealth generators." He does not know it, but he is rephrasing, in U.N.-speak, what Abdus Salaam told Doug Seebeck 20 years earlier: "In order to address the issue of poverty, we must get the rich involved with the poor. They have to become part of the solution."

When the time came to set up the affiliate, Mike Buwalda was the moving party from Partners Worldwide's main office. Paul Holwerda, president of Advantage Sign Supply, a computerized sign-making equipment business, agreed to be the North American Philippine affiliate (NAPA) team leader.

Paul threw his hat in because of a question that was pestering him: How can I become more personally involved in mission work? His business had grown to

He was searching for a mission in which to invest not only his money, but his skills.

60 employees. Although he had faithfully supported his church and his denomination, he was searching for a mission in which to invest not only his money, but his skills.

Providentially, Mike Buwalda approached Paul, asking him if he would be willing to show two Filipino businesspeople around his facility and explain the basis for its success. Several weeks after meeting them, Mike called Paul again and asked if he would be willing to go to the Philippines to help e-BEST get off the ground.

"Asia was the last place I ever wanted to visit," Paul admits. But he went. He discovered that he liked the people, found their vision compelling, and would be called upon to do what he loved best: mentoring and serving others.

Much to Paul's surprise, a few months later a buyer offered him a price he could not refuse for Advantage Sign Supply. At age 42 he found himself unexpectedly and unintentionally retired. He didn't know it then, but God was sweeping the decks clean for him. In a few years Paul would need to be free of all business distractions to provide leadership through some very turbulent waters.

Troubling Developments

For five years the operating fund of e-BEST was to be provided by CRWRC. Its Business Development Fund (BDF) of 10 million pesos ($212,000) was to be raised by members' savings and the Partners Worldwide Global Fund. The BDF was to be lent to qualified e-BEST members at 14% interest at a time when established credit institutions were averaging over 25%. It was calculated that the 10 million pesos could be raised in five years, at which point the organization would be sustainable.

A dynamic and visionary General Secretary (GS) for e-BEST was appointed in 2002. By June 2005 e-BEST had seven chapters with about 200 members. The following year it had grown to 17 chapters with about 400 members, and the BDF had reached nearly 8 million pesos ($169,000).

In July, Tito Contado was called out of retirement by the Asian Development Bank to help them following the tsunami in Indonesia, so Tito stepped down from e-BEST's board. The newly-elected officers were inexperienced in board administration, and they all lived several hours away from the headquarters in Manila. That meant that the management of e-BEST was almost completely dependent on the GS. Although savings increased, the monitoring of operational expenses, loan disbursements, and loan collections became erratic. Trusting implicitly in the integrity of the GS, the new board members did not request vouchers for cash advances for "operational expenses."

In early 2006 Paul Holwerda noticed some gaping holes in e-BEST's financial statements. He was also troubled that the checklist for loan disbursals was no longer matching the established loan criteria. Two loans jumped out at him. One was used to build an addition on a home; the other had been made to a non-member "borrower."

When he dug a little deeper Paul discovered that, contrary to policy, the GS was the only person approving loans and the board president was only a figure-head. Paul traveled to the Philippines to express his concerns and reiterate the need for a loan-approval committee. Upon returning to Grand Rapids, he was told that the GS had convinced the committee that their input was unnecessary and had disbanded it.

Paul returned to the Philippines a few months later and explained that Part-ners Worldwide would not be able to provide additional matching funds until the accounting issues and board responsibilities were addressed. Neither the board nor the General Secretary agreed to make any changes. Paul began receiv-ing angry letters accusing him of having a patronizing, colonialist attitude of mis-trust toward the Filipinos. It was suggested that due to this "betrayal," perhaps the partnership should be dissolved. Though hurt by the reaction, Paul explained that he had great respect for them but was only acting as any good partner would by sharing his honest concerns.

Conflict and Resolution

When Tito returned from Indonesia in 2007 he was re-elected president of e-BEST's board. Within two weeks he began receiving insistent calls from debt collection agencies and members demanding to withdraw their savings. The GS blamed the cash shortage on Partners Worldwide for failing to provide more matching funds. Following the board meeting in February it became clear that both of e-BEST's bank accounts were nearly empty. This prompted the board to suspend activities. When the 2006 financial statement prepared by an external auditor was made public, it disclosed five major issues:

- Excess of expenses over revenue was 1.2 million pesos ($25,000).
- Cash advances and personal loans to the GS amounted to 600,000 pesos ($12,000).
- Seventy-seven percent of the loans were past due.
- The BDF had fallen from 7.9 million pesos ($167,000) to 3.7 million pesos ($78,000).
- e-BEST did not have a standard accounting system.

When the GS was confronted with this assessment, he stepped down. In his resignation letter he assumed full responsibility and promised to repay what was owed. After one year of nonpayment, criminal and civil actions were filed.

Doug and I made our visit when the final criminal judgment was imminent. I remember a key conversation in Tito's van, after a few visits with the Christian attorney handling the cases. We were discussing biblical principles of conflict resolution. I had been reading through the distinctives of Partners Worldwide and brought up the organization's explicit commitment to reconciliation. The simple question that forced the issue was, "How can we consider Partners to be an agent of reconciliation called to empower other transforming agents if we don't help reconcile our own brothers?"

It was agreed that based upon the words of Jesus in Matthew 18:15-17, the primary responsibility for resolution of this relational, ethical, and business breach needed to be placed in the hands of local church officials. Joe Lamigo, an elder in the GS's church; Rev. Nomer, his pastor; and Rev. Lawrence de los Trinos, the General Secretary of the Christian Reformed Church of the Philippines, took responsibility for arbitrating the dispute. Within a week a settlement was reached. It was agreed that the full monetary obligations would be repaid, along with attorney fees. A few days later, installment payments began.

So Much More

It was a long and draining two years for e-BEST, but especially for Paul, who bore the brunt of the rancorous dispute. He is saddened by the devolution of an organization that once was so strong and vital. E-BEST has shrunk to one full-time staffer and only two active chapters.

> "I saw for the first time how businesspeople can make a huge difference in community transformation."

But Paul has not given up on the vision that prompted his initial commitment. "Though e-BEST may never come back to what it was, it is an outstanding model. It provides something that businesspeople are longing for: personal engagement." And here he repeats what I hear from just about every North American partnership affiliate member: "It's a whole lot more rewarding to be personally involved

Tito Contado and Paul Holwerda

than to just give money." Paul speaks a little wistfully as he looks back on the impact this partnership has had on his life. "I saw for the first time how business-people can make a huge difference in community transformation."

I ask Paul how partnering with Filipino entrepreneurs changed him spiritually, and he shares a brief story. "I was on a street corner in Manila. I was with members of e-BEST, one of whom was a lady who had just lost her grocery business. In the middle of the capital city they gathered around and began to pray for her." Paul stops for a second. The memory is still so fresh that he has to catch his breath. "I felt the presence of the Holy Spirit like I never had before. It was so strong and powerful. It was like all the street noise, the traffic—everything stood still."

Paul was trying to describe something that cannot easily be described: the felt, close presence of God. Once you've experienced that, you never forget it. It is worth all the money from the sale of any company in the world. Like the MasterCard ads say, it's "priceless." And so it's no wonder Paul has not let go.

The natural way in which his Filipino partners live out their Christianity has rubbed off on Paul: "I have become a much stronger Christian. I talk about my faith a lot more openly. Now I will pray in social settings with business associates." These experiences also showed him he could play a significant role in extending God's kingdom. "They opened my eyes to how I can minister and be in business at the same time. My vision of how I can contribute domestically and internationally has grown exponentially."

"It was all about making money. But now I know there is so much more."

I have one more question for him: "What would you do differently with Advantage Sign Supply had you known then what you know now?" The answer is almost immediate; Paul has done some thinking about this. "I would be involved much more overtly in my employees' spiritual lives. I would provide the means for my employees to serve. I would have more in-depth conversations with them and would help those who were in trouble. And I would institute a chaplain program."

What he is saying is what I would later hear from a fruit farmer in the fruit orchards of Washington state. He is telling me that he would have been more of a pastor in his business. Had he done so, I dare say he would not have needed to hire a chaplain.

Paul is an honest man, so he continues, "It was all about making money. But now I know there is so much more." He looks away at the waters of the lake that are rippling in the sunlight, where my youngest son is fishing with his. "I was so challenged by the example of my Filipino brothers." I take note that Paul has not called them "partners." That is what partnering across the ocean with those who share a passion to use business as ministry inevitably does, despite the hardships and disappointments. This successful businessman has experienced the power of reciprocal transformation.

The Vision Lives

Though the story of e-BEST was discouraging, when Doug Seebeck and I visited other businesses in the Philippines, it became clear that the vision that inspired e-BEST is alive and well.

Bendix and Cora Chan began a healthcare business in the 1990s. Their purpose was to use their profits to provide for pastors who could not afford the high costs of medical care. The business was growing quickly, but in 2004 their partner embezzled 76 million pesos (more than $1.5 million), and the Chans were forced to close their business down. Like e-BEST, they had to learn the painful lesson (impossible without the Holy Spirit's help) of forgiving others as Christ Jesus had forgiven them. As a result, they were freed from bitterness, though they are still repaying their bank for the embezzled funds. Though it was difficult, God used the experience of financial failure to open their eyes to the needs of the majority in their country who are borrowers, not savers.

Out of this painful experience, the Chans launched David Daniels International Services Company, Inc. DD, as they affectionately call the company, serves the flood of "OFWs" (Overseas Filipino Workers) who leave the country every day for jobs in the West. It provides financing for the application and help in preparing the documents. But the Chans have a larger agenda. Their company provides life and health insurance but, more importantly, trains the workers for success in their new work environments. And, using the principles of Crown Financial Ministries, it teaches them how to wisely use the money they will earn. Besides teaching Christian financial management principles, DD enrolls the workers in a mandatory savings program. The Chans estimate that they have been able to help more than 10,000 OFWs, and through their lending agency, Eastern Eagle Financing Corp., have provided more than 1,000 loans at below-market rates.

Cora Chan is a firecracker of a lady who bursts with excitement. She is on a single-minded mission to "provide financial emancipation" to her countrymen. After hearing Partners Worldwide's philosophy of providing matching funds rather than "giving money away," Cora volunteered to join the board of e-BEST.

We also met Marlane Villa-Real, president and CEO of Buena Mano Crafts, Inc. She decided to teach the squatters living outside her gated-community to make crafts, table runners, and Christmas ornaments. Marlane found outlets to market the products, and soon the largest Philippine craft store began to carry her goods. After reading an article about exportation, Marlane registered her new company, Buena Mano ("Good Hand"—which can refer to both high quality and good luck). Her first order was for $50,000. Soon her products were being carried by Macy's, Bloomingdale's, Abraham Strauss, Neiman Marcus, and Harrods of London, whose upscale buyers loved her ornate "baroque" ornaments.

Before the U.S. economy began to falter, she was employing over 1,000 uneducated and "unemployable" women. She now has 20 women in her factory and 200 making crafts at home. Marlane is an ardent evangelist who is committed to sharing Christ with her employees. She believes that most of them have come to know Jesus through working for Buena Mano. Before we leave, Marlane agrees to consider joining the board of e-BEST. Doug and I smile at each other. Things are looking up for Partners Worldwide's Philippine affiliate.

"A Burden for Our People"

I am once again struck by the level of commitment evidenced by my brothers and sisters overseas. They serve Christ through their businesses in the marketplace, and most are also devoted to mentoring others. Tito Contado speaks for so many when he tells us, "I have a burden for our own people." That is why he remains committed to e-BEST.

> "Success in business is not measured by how much you make but how much you have helped others advance God's kingdom in the world."

He and Lou have taken on some other burdens as well. In the Philippines, microenterprises and small retailers are often prey to predatory lenders who charge nearly 120% interest annually. The Contados began buying out these usurious loans and charging substantially lower interest. They also instituted a savings program. Of the 30 vendors they helped in one year, they helped three entrepreneurs become financially free.

Tito tells me that the choice to pour his energies into building an enterprise aimed at the production of helpful goods and services, creating jobs for the poor and unemployed, and mentoring others to do the same "has totally transformed my life."

Had he decided to spend his remaining years at his desk and on the golf course where he used to enjoy many quiet, uninterrupted hours, he would have missed out on so much. He also would never have been able to model and teach this most crucial lesson: "Success in business is not measured by how much you make but how much you have helped others advance God's kingdom in the world."

Upon our return to the United States, Doug and I received an update on the settlement of the financial issues with e-Best's former General Secretary. Payments were being made and all claims had been officially withdrawn. Further, Tito informed the board that he would guarantee the balance of the debt if the GS failed to follow through on the agreement. The message from the board was as short as it was sweet: "Based on this act of grace, e-BEST can move forward to the next chapter of our journey."

The Philippines: Reflections by Doug Seebeck

Years ago, when I was wrestling with how to discern God's voice more clearly, a wise mentor suggested, "Try to get in God's Word every day, and spend at least 30 minutes alone with God. It's like any other relationship; you need to be one on one, heart to heart, to start to hear each other."

We felt compelled to go to the Philippines, I am quite sure, because God knew that our brothers and sisters there needed more than a few words by email or phone. We needed to *be there*, to be present face to face.

For me, the Philippines was a bittersweet country to visit. It is beautiful, dynamic, and filled with some of the most gracious people on earth. It is also home to a once-thriving business organization that has been reduced to a shadow of what it once was.

It's fair to say that e-BEST has gone through the greatest challenge of any of our international business affiliates. In retrospect, I wonder why I didn't visit with its leaders earlier, given the depth of their frustration and discouragement. It's not easy to sense the reality of someone's pain if you're not looking them in the eyes. Regardless, I still marvel at the number of answered prayers—and yes, miracles—that we experienced.

Joetique ("Joe") Lamigo is a colleague and dear friend. He is one of the best in the business of community organizing and transformation. He is also the team leader for CRWRC in the Philippines, and a social entrepreneur. When I explained the vision of Partners Worldwide to Joe in 1998, he picked up on it immediately and began to organize. Because he recognized the strategic importance of bridging the gap between rich and poor, he intentionally began identifying business leaders in communities where he had credibility and experience. He looked for entrepreneurs with vision, a heart for the poor, and a mind for business.

When Partners Worldwide began, it was part of the organizational structure of CRWRC in the Philippines. After several years it became clear to both organizations that our partnership could achieve much more if we separated our administrative functions and focused on our respective core strengths. We would still collaborate, but as two independent entities. That freed us to focus on the growing numbers of businesspeople in the Philippines and throughout the developing world who needed to be served in the same way as our North American members.

As the field leader representing the partnership for CRWRC, Joe played a crucial role in building the capacity of e-BEST and formalizing its management and governance systems. When the organizational separation took place, Joe handed off his responsibilities to the newly appointed director of e-BEST. Shortly thereafter, Tito was called away to work with the World Bank on a project in Indonesia, and a leadership and accountability vacuum was created that precipitated e-BEST's organizational deterioration. In a perfect world, it might have worked out. In our imperfect world, we did not realize that we had created the perfect storm.

Peter Drucker, the social ecologist and management theorist, used to wisely remind his readers that all our best-laid plans must eventually degenerate into hard work. My mentor, Rich DeVos, the founder of Amway Corporation, has stressed the importance of showing up for work every day and paying attention to business, one foot in front of the other, even when it gets boring. Nothing can substitute for accountability, supervision, communication, and working shoulder to shoulder. In retrospect, it is clear that we took our eyes off the ball in e-BEST's case.

I'm very glad Tim and I went to the Philippines. It is obvious now, though we didn't know it as we were flying toward Asia, that we were being sent on a mission of reconciliation. We had no clue that God had bigger plans for us than getting good quotes for a book and encouraging tired brothers and sisters. We did not come over with clever strategies and quick fixes to share with the board members. When we sat around the table with them, we didn't flick open our laptops and download seven sure-fire principles for success and prosperity. Life is hard. Business is tough. And sometimes things get very messy. So we listened a lot. We took notes. We hugged and affirmed those who had been in the thick of things and had grown very weary. It was important for us to look them in the eyes and grieve with them in their discouragement.

When we spoke, what we shared with them was hope. We came with fresh eyes and an open heart and were astonished to find, in the words of Jesus, that the fields were "white and ready for harvest." Because we came from outside the whirlpool of struggle, we were able to identify some wonderful opportunities that were right there, ready to be mined.

Time and again, what we found most impacting were the moments we gathered around a table and prayed together. We so easily forget that what we all need more than anything is Jesus. We exhaust ourselves fighting the battles on our own strength. The apostle Paul made it very plain that prayer tears down enemy strongholds (which, in the e-BEST context, were fear, discouragement, blame, and anger). But prayer also serves to build us up in faith, in hope, and in love.

It was as a result of prayer that deeply estranged brothers were reconciled and a vital international partnership given new life. E-BEST has passed through the valley of shadow and death. But they will fear no evil, for they have been reminded that they are not alone—God is with them and so are we.

One of the six core values Partners Worldwide shares is a commitment we've taken from Winston Churchill: "Never, never, never give up!" Our tenacity is not premised on innate stubbornness, but on our unshakable confidence in Christ's renewing, reconciling power. We are convinced that he who has begun a good work in his people will bring it to full maturity on the day when all things in heaven and earth will be reconciled to him.

We came back from our trip to the Philippines with memories of creativity, giftedness, commitment, and competence. We also returned with the sense that e-BEST still has a bright future and the best is yet to come.

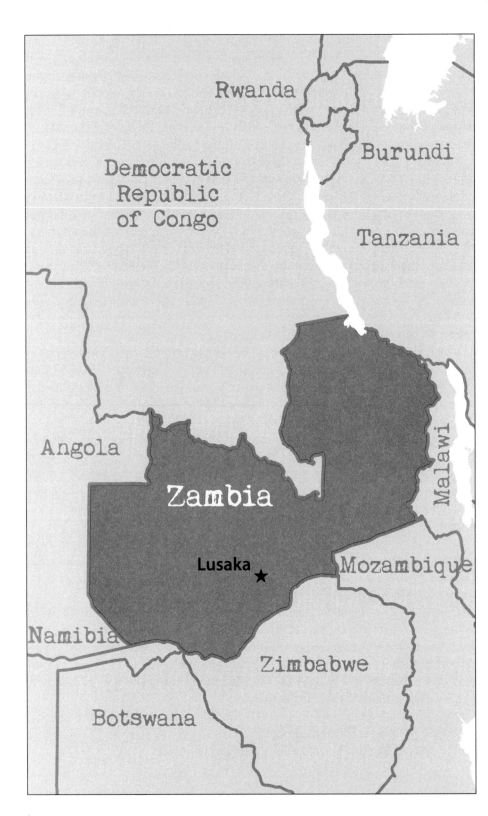

Zambia and North America

The Context

BY DOUG SEEBECK

The final leg of our journey to visit partners around the world takes us to Zambia. In these stories you'll read of transformation not only in Africa, but in North America as well. Partners Worldwide is called to promote reconciliation, to establish relationships that result in reciprocal transformation among the poor *and* the rich. What we have learned in our 10 years is that if we wish to impact the world, we must be impacted ourselves. We must live the change we wish to see. These final stories, while they have roots in the country of Zambia, also show us that reconciliation must begin at home.

When my family and I returned to the U.S. from Africa in the summer of 1996, one of the first places we visited was Sunnyside, Washington. My parents still attended Sunnyside Christian Reformed Church, a solid church in a hardworking farming community whose congregation had faithfully been praying, encouraging, and financially supporting first me, and then our family, since 1978. I was eager to thank them for their faithful support and share the exciting vision for an organization of business partnerships.

After the service, I invited Jerry Haak and some other farmers to a breakfast meeting to talk about some opportunities for their personal involvement in this brand-new organization. At that time, CRWRC had an agriculture extension program in eastern Zambia. My question for these farmers was whether they would be willing to launch the first-ever Farmer to Farmer (F2F) partnership. I explained that the costs for the project would not be covered by their church's budgeted mission support; rather, as part of their commitment they would be responsible for raising the necessary resources from their agriculture business network.

Although the farmers were initially a little skeptical, they eventually agreed. That's what I love about entrepreneurs. They carefully weigh the needs and the options in front of them, and then they decide.

One year into that new partnership, Jerry called me with a lead. Dr. Suzanne Baristow had just returned from a service stint in Kenya. She was the daughter of Ralph and Cheryl Broetje, who own and operate the largest privately-held fruit orchard in the world, which happened to be located about 90 minutes from Sunnyside. "Since you lived in Kenya all those years," Jerry suggested, "you should call the Broetjes up and make the connection. They could be good donors for Partners Worldwide. In fact, they could fund this entire operation in Zambia all by themselves."

I made the call. Not too long afterward, I met the Broetjes at their remarkable orchard. I was amazed. It was a business-ministry operation the likes of which I had never seen before. During that visit, our lives became intertwined as we discovered the similarities of our respective journeys, shared values, and vision for the potential power of business for kingdom good.

Some time later I received another phone call. This time it was from Gary Edmonds, who was then serving as the director of Churches Together, a young organization formed on behalf of a consortium of large churches committed to partnering to combat the HIV/AIDS crisis in Africa.

Gary and I had been discussing how Partners Worldwide might serve the businesspeople in their network, connecting their skills and expertise in creating jobs in those communities economically devastated by HIV/AIDS. He asked if I would be willing to meet with an entrepreneur named Benedict Schwartz, who had shared an unusual vision with him. It was a unique and demanding proposal that he felt required the expertise of a network of businesspeople like ours.

One of the core values of Partners Worldwide is intentional collaboration. We are passionate about our vision and mission and will try to work with anyone who shares our desire to see business and ministry work together. A few weeks later, Benedict, Gary, and I were sharing our stories and experiences in a Grand Rapids, Michigan, hotel. We were testing the waters, trying to determine whether God wanted us to work together. The experience bonded us and we agreed to take the next step, which would require meeting with the North American Zambian partnership team.

That meeting took place in early November at a retreat center in the mountains west of Seattle. Benedict shared his vision for "Villages of Hope" for abandoned orphans in Zambia and outlined an impressive entrepreneurial model for sustainability. At the end everyone agreed to introduce Benedict to the leaders of Christian Business with Integrity (CBI), our affiliate in Lusaka.

Benedict took his first trip to Zambia in December 2005. Six months later, a new partnership was formalized and a new model for orphan care with a strong entrepreneurial foundation began.

Benedict and Kathleen Schwartz

Remembering the Orphan

BY TIMOTHY STONER

B enedict Schwartz has a strong, ruddy face and burly arms. His eyes are brown, and there is a lot going on behind them. Though balding, he has a shock of white hair that looks a bit like Einstein's. In his former life he was the CEO of Dayspring, Inc., a small software company in Maryland. Behind his somewhat formidable facade is a heart that is pliable and has been gripped by the needs of abandoned children. He has allowed the cry of the orphan to penetrate and to break him.

It happened unexpectedly and, he will admit, inconveniently, as he read a magazine article that left him completely undone. It was about the daily struggles of street children in Brazil. As he sat in his leather office chair, he found himself crying. The question that kept welling up within him was, "God, isn't there anything we can *do*?" The answer he received was as provocative as it was startling: "Just like a family can sponsor a child, a church can sponsor a village." This answer was not anything Benedict would have dreamed up on his own; but he was certain God had given him clear marching orders.

The Schwartzes' church was involved in Africa, and through providential circumstances was offered free land in Namibia for an orphanage. That's how this Jewish software developer embarked on his mission to help orphans find hope and the possibility of a productive future.

Benedict is now in the process of building a second Village of Hope. This one is located in Zambia. I'm not at all certain what to make of this project, which from what I've heard seems to embrace much of the weaknesses of the traditional orphan-care system. The institutional orphanage model, though providing real benefits, has also been responsible for creating a welfare mentality in Africa. By taking children off the family land—which in Africa is everything—orphanages frequently leave children without the ability to make a living in agricultural regions that have high unemployment. What I call the "relief-based" model is dependent upon large infusions of capital to build Western-style structures that require a stream of outside funds and foreigners to direct, manage, and maintain. Failing to begin with an end-strategy has locked in a cycle of paternalism and co-dependence.

Although this is troubling, what is even more pressing is this question: What does an orphan village have to do with business: income generation, employment, economic growth, and financial independence? There is no doubt that Benedict is on a wonderful and compelling mission of mercy, but if it does not lead to business growth and is not sustainable, I realize that it is antithetical to Partners Worldwide's distinctive.

Before leaving to interview Benedict I heard some criticism about the capital expenditures required to build this small community. Having met Benedict at an orphan conference years earlier, I hold on to the hope that this entrepreneur is not going to replicate the old model. I also know that Benedict spent quite a bit of time with Doug Seebeck before launching the project. From what I have gathered, they had some "robust dialogue" about sustainability. I'm anxious to see how Benedict's model and the vision of Partners Worldwide have meshed.

An "On-Ramp"

As we begin our trek around the 230-acre parcel, my fears begin to dissipate. The land was provided by three Christian "aunties" who wanted to help care for local orphans. Rather than building an institutional structure, Benedict chose to implement a village concept. Village of Hope is composed of three-bedroom houses, each of which is home to eight orphans and one house mother, a widow who has been carefully trained to care for multiple children. Benedict's plans include building a total of 26 houses to shelter about 200 orphans.

The ratio of caregivers to orphans is excellent (I have been in orphanages where 50 orphans to one caregiver was the norm), but this is a capital-intensive venture. Each house costs around $28,000 to build, up from the $20,000 required for the first one two years earlier. The jump in cost is mainly attributable to cement prices, which have more than quadrupled. Once the houses are finished it takes about $550 to cover the monthly expenses. Churches and individuals are beginning to step forward to shoulder those ongoing costs. Benedict believes that this provides the North American church with a wonderful "on-ramp" to fulfill the biblical imperative to care for orphans and widows in their distress.

As we continue our walking tour around the compound, I feel a growing excitement. What I recognize in short order is that the Village of Hope has compassion *and* business as its twin propulsion engines. This is unlike any of the orphanage models I have known. The orphans receive excellent care from their caregivers, but what pays the bills is the village's innovative income-generating commitment.

The Village of Hope has compassion and business as its twin propulsion engines.

As Benedict points out various crops that are growing, new foundations being laid, and the locations of future entrepreneurial ventures, he also tells me how this vision had its birth.

From Maryland to Namibia to Zambia

Benedict and his wife, Kathleen, were living a comfortable, successful and fulfilling life. In 1985 he started Dayspring, a company that specialized in software for schools and organizations working with disabled people. The Schwartzes were active members of Mt. Zion United Methodist Church in Bel Air, Maryland. Kathleen was their music director. A gifted administrator and innovative musician, she had formed five music teams and a choir. She also owned and directed, with two partners, a music school for 400 students. They were both quite content with their life, which included caring for their six children, four biological and two adopted, until reading that fateful article.

Kathleen and Benedict Schwartz

On 17 donated acres in Namibia they built their first Children of Zion Orphan Village. Today, it is home to 57 orphans. One of the children, Albert, had been sold to an extended family member and was working as the family's personal slave. When Benedict found him he was being forced to live inside a truck tire in the back yard and had almost died several times from malaria.

After a few years Benedict began to feel persistent nudges to build another village. The Schwartzes settled on Zambia, partly because he had heard that one in ten children living there were orphans, but also because he learned that a decade earlier the country had declared itself a "Christian nation." That meant that there were no restrictions on teaching children about Jesus in the local schools. The biggest incentive was an offer of free land. (God is aware how irresistible this is for North Americans. It worked perfectly.)

In December 2005, after meeting with the Partners Worldwide team for Zambia, Benedict went on a scouting expedition to survey the property in a remote area in the north. There was no water, no electricity, and no good roads. Benedict had determined early on that those three components were essential for the new orphan village. "This is what creates so much difficulty for Christian ministries," he tells me. "Land is so valuable in the West that North Americans will take land anywhere if it is free."

> His home was inside a truck tire in the back yard.

Here Benedict betrays his innate good sense: "Land in Africa is not like in America. In Africa, 80% of the land is not being used. There are chiefs in every village who are more than willing to provide prime property if it means the economic betterment of their tribe. We didn't need to accept the first thing that came along just because it was being given at no cost." This is when I decide to begin calling him "Big Bwana," because I recognize that he has the gift of wisdom as well as administration.

Benedict began looking for a strategic piece of real estate. He found it along the Great North road—the best-maintained and busiest transportation artery in the nation. It bisects Zambia, providing access to South Africa in the south and Tanzania in the north.

Benedict, entrepreneur that he is, was thinking about income-generation at the same time as he was thinking about orphans. He wanted to provide the orphans with indigenous strategies to ensure that they would be free from economic dependence. What he had in mind was a new paradigm of orphan-care that would be sustainable and replicable throughout the continent.

A Family Business

The idea had been prompted by a phrase that had invaded Benedict's mind during the construction of the Children of Zion village in Namibia. As he was standing in that village, bathed in the golden African sunlight and watching dozens of orphans laughing and playing, a new imperative pierced him: "Make every provision for these kids that you do for your own children." Benedict intuitively knew that this meant one certain thing: the orphans needed to grow up in the context of a family business.

Benedict was raised helping his father in the family furniture store. He subscribes to the ancient model in which parents give their children love as well as hands-on training in business. Benedict shares his unique perspective with me: "What orphans lose in Africa and around the world is not only the nurture of parents, but the incredible benefit of growing up in and around business. Without a father at home, they are often raised without the example of hard daily work and the spirit of entrepreneurship."

This is something I had not thought of before. My parents were missionaries and their job was starting churches, not growing businesses. But I get the point immediately. "Children who grow up in such environments learning about finances from their parents have a huge leg up on most others who lack it," Benedict says. "As a result, orphans suffer a double loss and are often irreparably handicapped in terms of learning to fend for themselves."

Three Good Ideas

The sanity and beauty of this model is made even more apparent to me on one particular morning of my visit. I am sitting in a circle of people in a square structure in the middle of the compound. The roof is thick, brown thatch. The walls are waist-high and built from about a thousand interlocking bricks, each one made from five parts red clay dirt and one part cement. The older orphans, most of whom were unemployed until recently, compressed the bricks by hand or by using a rented brick-making machine. It is one of several businesses that the village has launched.

I've joined the weekly meeting of the village's senior staff. There are ten members: six are Zambian support staff, two are the orphan-care directors (Francis Kamau, a Kenyan, himself an orphan; and Kimberly, his African American wife); the other two are Benedict and Kathleen. The Schwartzes represent only two out of the ten votes. Benedict explains why: "Not only are the Zambians carrying authority and responsibility, through these meetings they are learning how to manage a business."

At the very efficient meeting run by Francis, progress on each item from last week's minutes is tracked. One of longest agenda items relates to "the Market"—a roadside store that sells produce grown by older orphans on a farm cooperative they own and manage. The Market is the orphan village's primary income generator. Since the farm is just getting started, it is not yet producing all that is required to keep the shelves stocked, so the balance of the goods are bought at wholesale at nearby farms.

There is discussion about last week's decision to form a subcommittee to recommend methods to make the Market more profitable. In the process, creative ideas begin germinating. I count three excellent proposals that I know will find good soil. None of them were Benedict's. He later shares with me what a relief it is not to be the one looked to for all the money-generating strategies.

Miriam Sinkala, a widow in charge of training the other house mothers, makes the first suggestion. She used to run a small landscaping business. One day when she was beautifying the exterior of the market she was asked by several customers if they could buy the greenery and flowers she was planting. "Why not grow flowers and decorative plants and add that to what we sell at the store?" she says. In Lusaka, palm plants come two to a pot, she explains. "We can begin by buying them, selling one, and planting the other on the farm."

Another person proposes that since a Community Center is going to be built 15 yards away from the restaurant, why not (along with free books and Internet) put in some laminators and copiers that can be used for a fee by the teachers of the 20-some small schools in the area? He explains, "This will save them the transportation costs, and will be cheaper than what they already pay at a greater distance."

In addition to these new ideas, several other improvements have already been implemented. Plans are in place for a food processing facility behind the Market. Very soon a new restaurant will serve chicken and fish with "chips." The meat will be produced on site. The fish, tilapia, will be raised in two ponds being prepared for that very purpose. Chickens will also be raised on the cooperative's property.

The third idea suggested during the weekly meeting is my favorite. Mr. Phiri, who supervises the workers, observes that the tired truckers coming in for a meal will want to freshen up and relieve themselves. "Why don't we put in bathrooms that will be available for a small fee?" I get it immediately: *nice, clean bathrooms.* Even if the truckers don't find them irresistible, the *muzungu*, white tourists unaccustomed to Africa's restroom deficits, will—that I can flat-out guarantee.

Chickens for Sustainability

Benedict is not an agrarian, nor is he a contractor, though he has had to become quite conversant in both skill sets. Benedict is a networker. That, I come to believe, may be the most important skill one needs in order to replicate a Village of Hope. The "Big Bwana" has been in some negotiations and has won certain promises for the orphans and their economic future.

For example, the Zambian Youth Empowerment Trust (ZYET) has agreed to pay for the construction of two chicken runs on the Older Orphan Cooperative. Six thousand chickens will live in each run. It takes two months to fatten up the chicks, so that means six cycles of "broilers," or 72,000 chickens, per year. That income will go directly to the cooperative's members. Among other things, the money will be used for further education.

Because there is a chicken shortage in Zambia, ZYET will also be providing funds to construct six more chicken runs on acreage not being used by the village. ZYET will purchase the initial 6,000 chicks for each, which translates to 216,000 broilers per year. ZamBeef, a nearby meat and poultry processor, needs to process a million chickens per year, and is falling short, so they have offered to buy all the chickens the Village of Hope can raise. The profit on each bird is 30 cents. This will provide the village with an income stream that will far exceed operational costs. *That* is what is known as sustainability.

There are currently nine students, most of whom are older orphans, who are being trained by Joseph Mkangala, an agriculturalist on staff. During the first year of their two-year curriculum, the students learn about conservation farming—the labor-intensive but highly efficient method of hand-watering and hand-fertilizing only the actual plants themselves, as opposed to the common but more wasteful system of using expensive sprinklers to indiscriminately shower precious water resources over broad areas. In places where unemployment rates are high, laborers are plentiful, and natural resources are both expensive and limited, conservation farming is a superior technique.

In their second year the apprentice agriculturalists will learn how to raise chickens—lots of them.

The Chimwemwe Ladies' Club

Another example of economic empowerment was displayed later that same afternoon. That is when the Chimwemwe Ladies' Club met. It comprises approximately 30 women from the community, many of whom are widows. They meet in the same hut where the leadership team gathers to strategize money-making ventures.

They begin by singing songs of worship. Several women who cannot contain their happiness stand up to dance. After about half an hour, some women bring out large stacks of the colorful plastic bags used by retail stores. The Ladies' Club members begin cutting the bags into strips about 3 inches wide. The resulting hoops of plastic are cut and carefully knotted together to form long strands of varying colors. Then the women thread the strands through their fingers and begin expertly crocheting them into women's handbags.

It takes two to three days to finish a bag. The bags, priced at $20, are sold to visitors, volunteers, and churches in North America. The ladies have also learned how to make wrap-around skirts from traditional African cloth. To help out the Westerners, who don't know how to tie the skirts so they don't come undone at awkward moments, the women sew on long ties. This, I decide, is a socially and commercially wise sartorial improvement.

That evening I am let in on the next phase of development for the Ladies' Club. "As it happens," Benedict says, "a short-term missionary is coming soon to work with our children. She wasn't sure what she had to offer, since she is not a nurse or a teacher. I asked her what she had studied and she told me, a little sheepishly, that she had just graduated with a degree in clothing design." Benedict grins. "I told her she will have plenty to do. She will be teaching the ladies how to make uniforms for our workers and for the children. She was so excited to know that she will be training widows to be seamstresses able to start sewing businesses in their community." This is just one more economic spin-off from an orphan village that is really functioning as a small-business incubator.

"Not an Option"

What I became convinced of during the few days I was at the Orphan Village is that Benedict is no believer in the traditional, dependent, institutional model of orphan care. To put it into the starkest economic terms, he and Kathleen are launching an experiment in creative, compassionate capitalism. Switching over to biblical language, I would say they are pioneers modeling one of the healthiest and most effective ways for the church to fulfill its God-given orphan-care imperative. The church not only is *responsible* to care for orphans, it *needs* to care for orphans. This is Benedict's conviction, and I could not agree more.

On our last full day in Zambia, Benedict and I sit together inside a large gazebo under a thatched roof supported by 6-inch tree trunks. The weather is perfect: temperatures in the low 80s F, clear blue sky, a slight breeze, and low humidity. Benedict admits that he sometimes feels he has one of the cushiest assignments in Africa, at least weather-wise. We are finishing up an English breakfast provided by the cook who runs the African "bed and breakfast" where I have been staying with my oldest son, Jonathan.

The night before, Benedict and I had talked about replicability: "Nice model, friend, but can it really be repeated widely? Isn't it a bit expensive? Doesn't it require a highly specialized skill set?"

Today he informs me that he has been thinking about these questions. "The problem of and the solution for replicability is not money, but people," he says, rather cryptically. "I didn't know anything about farming," he explains. "The extent of my knowledge was planting a beet in the backyard when I was a kid. I have no experience in construction, either. What I do have is the ability to think, to network, to motivate others. And, though I am not wealthy myself, I know others who are."

He looks up after finishing the last of the fried eggs and grilled tomato. "There are thousands like me—and like you," he asserts, including me in

> The church not only is responsible to care for orphans, it needs to care for orphans.

the pool of agricultural and architectural incompetents. I nod; I know nothing about those fields either.

Although we've been talking about serious matters, the tone has been light. Suddenly, Benedict becomes very sober and looks at me with his intelligent and thoughtful eyes. I can tell he's getting ready to unload something important. "People think that it is such a wonderful thing for me to be building houses for orphans. They act like it is a nice option, that I am doing something heroic. I'm not. What they don't understand is that it is not an option, for them or for me. I am taking care of orphans for the sake of my soul."

"The issue of replicability lies in whether people are willing to obey the biblical command to care for orphans in their distress."

After letting that sink in, he continues, again on the theme of replicability. "The problem is not the cost. The Lord has all the money that is needed to provide for the orphans of the world. The issue of replicability lies in whether people are willing to give their lives and use the skills they have to obey the biblical command to care for orphans in their distress. Or—" he stops to mull over his conclusion—"will they choose instead to go on an extended vacation when they retire?" It's a very important question, and I wonder what I will decide in 20 years or so.

On the flight back I think about how Benedict's model is ideal for entrepreneurs. It's a perfect blend of risk, creative enterprise, commerce, and compassion. Granted, it requires a lot of start-up capital to build a community like Village of Hope. But it might be a lot more costly *not* to.

Ken Whitmire

"Dream dreams to bless others."

Jerry and Rosie Haak
Marketplace Ministers

BY TIMOTHY STONER

On Wall Street the winner is the one who manages funds best, but in the "fruit basket" of Washington state, whoever manages sunlight best wins. Fruit farmer Jerry Haak explains: "If you can get sunlight to every leaf, you will beat the competition. The tree is talking to you, and what you have to do is manipulate the branches so they can be more fruitful than they would be otherwise." I have spoken with many different kinds of managers in my travels, but talking with a "sunlight manager" is a first. I am in the home of 46-year-old Jerry and his wife, Rosie, in Outlook, Washington. On their 550 acres they grow apples, pears, and cherries.

Jerry calls sunlight "the last unregulated natural resource in the Western world." He's successful because he has given the management of sunlight long and careful thought. He has designed systems to string and tie and pull and lever fruit tree branches for maximum sunlight and maximum production. He also has developed trees whose fruit is lower to the ground for easier picking, and he plants trees close together for maximum per-acre yield. Jerry says, "We produce up to 15 tons per acre on cherries, 25 tons per acre on pears, and up to 45 tons per acre on apples." In an

In an industry where 15-20 tons of apples per acre is considered a good yield, Jerry's numbers are outstanding.

industry where 15-20 tons of apples per acre is considered a good yield, Jerry's numbers are outstanding.

Treasure in Heaven

Jerry didn't grow up on an orchard. His father owned a mid-size dairy farm, but due to Jerry's ankylosing spondylitis, a painful and chronic arthritic disease, it was impossible for him to follow his father's footsteps. So he went to Dordt College in Iowa, got a degree in agricultural business, and took a job writing and collecting farm loans. He used his problem-solving skills and his gift of mercy to help restructure debts so farmers could stay on their farms. In the next six years he learned that though he loved helping others solve their financial difficulties, what he most wanted was to work for himself.

In 1986 he decided to try his hand at apples, despite having "absolutely no idea how to grow fruit." His strategy was simple: "I targeted four or five very successful farmers in the area and gave one of them a call every month with a long list of questions." To his surprise and delight, the farmers would spend almost an hour per month "giving away their trade secrets" to this young, inexperienced, but highly motivated fruit farmer. "It is because of their help that I have succeeded," Jerry says. He now has 25 full-time employees and 70 seasonal workers.

Rosie, Jerry's sweetheart since the sixth grade, was the valedictorian of her graduating class at nearby Sunnyside High School. In her graduation address, she spoke about the New Testament story of the rich young ruler and Jesus' call to store up treasure in heaven rather than on earth. As a result of her speech several of her class members committed their lives to Christ. When Rosie and Jerry branched out into tending orchards, they carried with them the determination to lay up treasure where it matters most.

They eventually decided to dedicate the profits from a portion of their ranch to God. The first year they set aside four acres. After harvesttime, they discovered that the yield from the "firstfruits" acreage exceeded that of all the others. Now they set aside 12 acres, with a profit of around $10,000 per acre.

> "Whenever we plant a new orchard, we go out to the barren field and ask God to bless the work we will do there."

Jerry explains to his children and his employees that since God is the one who blesses their crops every year, this is their way of saying thank you for his grace in their lives. "Whenever we plant a new orchard, we go out to the barren field and ask God to bless the work we will do there," he tells me. "I can say that God has blessed me more than I could have ever imagined." Today, through their work with Partners Worldwide, Jerry and Rosie are passing that blessing on.

Farmer to Farmer

Jerry's relationship with Doug Seebeck goes back a long way. Their families attended the same church in Sunnyside, Washington. When Doug returned to the United States in 1996 after 18 years in Bangladesh and East Africa, he began sharing the vision of creating partnerships between North American business-people and African entrepreneurs.

"Doug is very persuasive," Jerry smiles. Though he suspected that Doug's idea was a fundraising gimmick, he agreed to get involved in Partners Worldwide's work in Zambia. The Zambian "Farmer to Farmer" program was what intrigued him most. The purpose was to help farmers move from subsistence to food security. A three-year program would teach principles of crop rotation, irrigation, nitrogen-fixing, and raising fish. The end goal was for each farmer to have a food surplus, which could be sold to purchase necessities for their families.

> To date the Zambian Farmer to Farmer program has helped close to 22,000 families become self-sustaining.

This simple and inexpensive idea has been a resounding success, surpassing the most optimistic projections. Jerry tells me that, "to date, the Zambian Farmer to Farmer program has helped close to 22,000 families become self-sustaining. It has been so successful that the Canadian Food Resource Bank has even joined as a partner, contributing $100,000 per year."

The Christian Reformed World Relief Committee also wanted to encourage orphan care in the farm community, so they provided incentives (seed, fertilizer, or food) to families that would take in orphans. As a result of this assistance, more than 1,600 children robbed of parents by HIV/AIDS are now being cared for by their extended community.

Jerry's father, Henry Haak, did his part to help Zambian farmers too. When he visited their country he saw that the land was remarkably similar to Washington's Yakima Valley. He also noticed that the Zambians had irrigation difficulties. In order to provide water for their crops, they were relying on the ancient and inefficient method of hauling it up by hand, one bucket at a time. So Henry designed a simple water pump that could be produced from cheap local materials. Its components were a few feet of PVC pipe, rubber from a bicycle tire tube, and a plastic wafer with holes drilled in it. It cost around $15 to make and is still referred to as the "Henry Pump."

The Washington farmers also encouraged a revolutionary new farming paradigm: don't wait for the rainy season to plant. Instead, plant before it rains and irrigate the seedlings by hand. The theory is that it takes only a little water to get a seed to germinate, and when the rainy season begins the plants are sturdy enough to survive the downpours. By pre-irrigating the crops, the farmer hastens the harvest by one month. In a survival context that can be the difference between life and death. And in a commercial context, that means your crops are ready for market four weeks before those of your competitors.

Local Needs, Local Solutions

In 2005 Jerry was anxious to visit Zambia to see the work he had been financially supporting for more than nine years. However, when he showed up for his travel vaccines, the doctor explained that the regimen he was on to control the ankylosing spondylitis could cause him to become infected with the very diseases he was being inoculated against. In other words, getting the vaccines could kill him. Jerry returned home, realizing he would never be able to visit the farmers and children he had been helping in Zambia.

Instead of allowing the physical barrier to stop him, Jerry recruited his friend Don Weippert to go in his place. At that time Benedict Schwartz (see previous chapter) was considering the construction of the Village of Hope for Zambian orphans. Don put his experience as a businessman and farmer to use by helping Benedict evaluate the quality of the soil at three possible locations and providing counsel that resulted in refining and clarifying his orphan-care vision.

Partners Worldwide's Washington affiliate also brought two Zambian farmers to the U.S. to learn farming techniques firsthand. Eventually Justin Kadyeni became the local leader of the project overseeing thousands of farmers in his own country. Ernest Lusampa returned to Zambia with an expanded vision and encouragement to start a private for-profit school. Though the Washington affiliate was tempted to provide the funding for the school building, equipment, and materials, Lou Haveman of Partners Worldwide strongly encouraged the North Americans not to "lead with money."

They followed his advice and chose instead to carefully investigate and encourage local solutions. Eventually they provided an interest-free loan of $15,000 to build a four-room schoolhouse. In 2006 the Chipata Primary School began with six students. In less than two years the school has grown to approximately 100 students. Del Dykstra, superintendent of Washington's Sunnyside Christian School, spent six weeks in Zambia with his family to provide mentoring help to the teachers and administration.

Not everything has been a success, however. In 2003 Ernest Lusampa led the way in initiating the Chipata Savings and Loan. It was modeled after CHESS in Kenya, which matched the members' savings along with another matching grant from the Partners Worldwide Global Fund. In the Chipata Savings and Loan's first year, the Washington affiliate provided $18,000 in start-up funds, and eventually $54,000 was loaned out. But Jerry explains that "there have been repeated violations of the loan-making policies." A substantial amount was lent for short-term, personal, non-business reasons—and those funds were never repaid. To date, $34,000 of the initial loan moneys have been paid back, and there are about 25 loans outstanding. The default rate is hovering around 70%.

The Henry Pump Jerry's father designed is another source of frustration and disappointment. "There have been very few takers. Though it is efficient and cheap, it is human-energy intensive." (This means that it can use up more calories than are available in the Zambian farmers' current diet.) But what proved most intractable was the cultural barrier to new technology. So, for the time being, Zambian farmers continue to draw water out of wells using wooden or plastic pails. Not all innovations have been ignored, though; many farmers are benefitting nutritionally and financially from early planting and pre-irrigation.

There is great wisdom in allowing local needs to initiate local ideas that sprout into solutions that the Americans can partner with.

The failures have taught Jerry and others in the Washington affiliate a crucial lesson: there is great wisdom in allowing local needs to initiate local ideas that sprout into solutions that the Americans can partner with. "Imposing American solutions to African problems just does not work all that well." He shakes his head; it is still a hard pill to swallow. "What took the least money and the least work on our end [the Chipata school] has accomplished the best results." Jerry shrugs his shoulders. He'd love to see the Zambians irrigate more efficiently. "The pump was our idea," he says, "but the school was theirs." That, apparently, makes all the difference in the world.

What They Give Away

In 2006 Jerry attended a Partners Worldwide conference where two speakers affected him profoundly: Ed Silvoso, an Argentinian evangelist with an international ministry to business leaders, and Cheryl Broetje, an extremely successful fruit farmer from Pasco, Washington, about 80 miles from the Haak farm. They both spoke about the connection between work and worship. According to Jerry, "The Broetje farm is the best example of seamless integration of faith and business I've ever seen—anywhere." During these seminars Jerry heard a challenge that would drastically change his perspective as a business owner.

Cheryl Broetje had spoken with a boldness that was unexpected but convicting. "She suggested that we were just using the partnership model as a hobby," Jerry remembers. "She told us flat out, 'You don't want the poor mingling with you. You don't want anyone to mess with your social clubs.' And then she challenged us to ask ourselves, 'Is this international partnership work really my lifestyle, or is it just something I do on the side?'" Jerry returned to his farm with a commitment to run it as his mission by following the model developed by his neighbors, the Broetjes.

> "She told us flat out, 'You don't want the poor mingling with you. You don't want anyone to mess with your social clubs.'"

Ralph and Cheryl grow about 5,300 acres of apple trees and 50 acres of cherries. Theirs is the largest family-owned apple orchard in the world. They pack an average of 20,000 boxes of apples per day—enough to fill 25 trucks. Collectively their orchards are a $60 million business. But the money they make is not what is most significant—it's what they give away. Each year 50-75% of the orchards' profits are donated to the family's Vista Hermosa Foundation and to related ministries. In 2008, the foundation distributed more than $5 million in grants to international partners.

The Broetje Way

Broetje Orchards employs around 1,100 people, but during harvesttime this number swells by another thousand. Because many of their employees are migrant workers, the Broetjes were challenged to learn about the roots of systemic poverty and how to address the needs of the poor.

In 1986 the Broetjes opened the Center for Sharing, which promotes hope by encouraging marginalized people to begin dreaming dreams for their future. The center provides an environment in which they can explore God's call on their lives and consider, within a small group context, how to apply that call in ways that heal, reconcile, and free others for service. Out of these groups at least a score of local and international ministries have either been birthed or are currently being served.

The Broetjes also developed a residential community named Vista Hermosa ("Beautiful View"). It includes comfortable and affordable rental dwellings for 126 members of their orchard "family." The Orchard View Market provides the residents of Vista Hermosa with basic-need commodities, and some of the workers' older children have the opportunity to work at the market and learn business skills.

The Vista Hermosa community also offers ESL and GED courses along with computer learning, summer camps, youth programs, parenting training, athletics, counseling services, women's support groups, and WIC programs. To provide better care for their employees' children, the Broetjes built a preschool and an elementary school. A scholarship program provides college tuition for their employees' children.

The Cherry Committees

Because Ralph and Cheryl are also committed to developing the leadership gifts of their employees, they created an opportunity for employees to participate in funding projects. The Broetje Orchards Cherry Committees are managed and directed entirely by Broetje employees.

The committees' main funding source developed almost by accident. Hidden among the hundreds of thousands of apple trees is a 50-acre parcel devoted to cherries. In 1990, after seven years of losses on that parcel, Ralph had lost hope that it would ever become profitable. He decided to cut the cherry trees down and replace them with apples. But one day, while reading the gospels, he was forced to reconsider.

In the book of John there is an unusual parable about the owner of a vineyard with a dilemma just like Ralph's. In the midst of his productive orchard was a lone fig tree that had not borne fruit for three years. The owner's patience was finally exhausted. So, arms waving in the air, he barked out orders to cut the tree down. In the story, a field worker advocates on behalf of the miserable fig tree, begging the owner to give it one more chance. The owner responds, "If it bears fruit next year, fine! If not, then chop it to the ground" (John 13:9). The story leaves us hanging. We are not told whether the fig tree got its lifetime reprieve, but the implication is that it did.

As far as Ralph was concerned, he had received direct instructions: he was to give the recalcitrant cherries one more year. If they produced well, the proceeds—all of them—were to be given away. The beneficiary Ralph and Cheryl

He was to give the recalcitrant cherries one more year. If they produced well, then the proceeds—all of them—were to be given away.

selected was Pimpollo, the neediest orphanage in Mexico. It was little more than a decrepit warehouse filled with 100 severely disabled and maimed orphans.

"We have to take Jesus into every facet of our life—our business, our workplace—every area."

Several months after conveying this decision to Padre Pancho, the priest who directed the orphanage, the Broetjes received a letter from him. It read, "Ever since the children in our home heard about what you planned to do with the proceeds, they have been praying for the orchard. But they have no idea what a cherry is. Could you please send them pictures so that they can see what they are praying for?"

The Broetjes obliged, and pictures of the small red fruit were posted on the orphanage wall. The orphans prayed all through the fall and winter, and kept up through the harvest in July.

God heard the prayers of those little ones. In late October of 1991, the orphans at Pimpollo were informed that a draft in the amount of $350,000 had been sent to them from the profits of a fruit they had never seen or tasted. The Broetjes' 50-acre parcel of cherries had yielded the greatest per-acre profit in their orchards' entire history.

That's how the Cherry Committees project got its start. Recently, the Committees donated almost $400,000 to World Vision's work in Africa, and last year their total distributions topped $900,000. In the past 17 years the once-unproductive acreage has seen bumper crops in all but two seasons.

Transformation

This is the model that Jerry Haak decided to emulate following the Partners Worldwide conference in 2006. He returned to his cherry and apple orchard having embraced the calling to be a change agent committed to transforming not only his business but his community.

Echoing Cheryl Broetje's words, he says, "Transformation has to be a lifestyle—if it is only helping out the poor domestically or internationally, it is just a tithe or a hobby. We have to take Jesus into every facet of our life—our business, our workplace—every area."

Rosie joins the conversation again. "We tell ourselves, 'When I retire I can serve,' or 'When my kids are out of school I'll have time.' No! We have to serve God *now* with all that we are. Jesus has to weave through all our life. It all has to be about him."

Jerry adds, "I tended to focus on church, home, and school—what I call the 'three-legged-stool.' But I think we often forget that the purpose for the stool is milking the cow." It's clear he has decided not to pull any punches. "I was good at building stools and shitty at milking the cow," he admits. "My business was completely disconnected from my Christian life."

Jerry continues, "Transformation needs to take place *here* [in North America] maybe more than it needs to take place *there* [overseas]." This is the first interview I've conducted in which that particular sentiment has been shared. It is humbling and refreshing. And after visiting five of those "places over there," each trip more convicting and provoking than the last, I could not agree more. Jerry continues, "Over here, our time is our god. That needs to change. We need to give it all to him: our time as well as our work."

"*This* is kingdom work," Jerry explains as he points outside to the cherry trees that flank the spacious yard. "I don't work anymore so that I can give money to extend the kingdom. I am doing it in and through my business."

All this talk about transformation has had a very real internal effect on Jerry. His self-concept has been radically changed. "I see myself now more like a pastor than a business owner. And while my 'parish' begins on my farm, it extends out to Sunnyside."

> "I don't work anymore so that I can give money to extend the kingdom. I am doing it in and through my business."

Building Relationships

This new perspective led the Haaks to become more deeply involved in the struggles faced by their employees. The neighboring town of Sunnyside is a rural community of approximately 15,000 people. Seventy-five percent of the population is Hispanic, and racism and prejudice run deep. Gangs are on the rise, and the teen pregnancy rate is well over 25%.

The Haaks decided to bring their neighbors' struggle to their church and school communities, which were homogenously white. They invited Cheryl Broetje to speak at their Christian school's annual dinner. "She began asking some direct questions," Rosie explains. They were pointed and hard to ignore. "Is your Christian school a reflection of your community, or are you nurturing a Christian ghetto?" She did the math for them. "If 75% of your area is Hispanic and your school is 90% Anglo, what is that saying about you?"

Following this challenge, Jerry and Rosie decided to address the soaring public high school drop-out rate by initiating a Christian school scholarship program for the families of their field workers. This program would provide incentives for graduation as well as assistance with college tuition. The goal of the fund was to put Christian education within the reach of Hispanic families.

But their involvement in Zambia with Partners Worldwide had taught them an important principle: "You don't just throw money at people—you have to build relationships." So they paired each scholarship student with a strong student-mentor. As it turned out, one of their own daughters was selected to be a mentor. When the mentoring relationship turned into a friendship, Rosie recalls how odd it was the first time the cultural/relational line was crossed. "I had never before had an employee child swimming in the family pool," she admits. Transformation can be a bit of a shock to the system.

Marketplace Ministers

Spurred on by the success of the scholarship program, Rosie and Jerry wanted to do more. Herm TeVelde, a retired farmer and a member of their church, had been to Zambia twice. He and Jerry decided to team up to teach a series of Sunday school lessons written by Ed Silvoso titled "Anointed for Business." The message was straightforward: as a Christian you are called to be a "pastor" of whatever area of responsibility God has given to you in the world. At the end of the class, the challenge was simple: "Will you commit to seeking spiritual and social transformation for our city?" Twenty-five individuals took up that challenge, and an initiative called Transformation Sunnyside was born.

> As a Christian you are called to be a "pastor" of whatever area of responsibility God has given to you in the world.

After the class Jerry and Herm distributed copies of Silvoso's book and sponsored city prayer meetings with local pastors and businesspeople. A core group of 14 leaders developed, and in November 2007 a city-wide meeting was held at the local high school. In the auditorium were 400 to 500 people representing about 30 churches. At the commissioning service Ed Silvoso brought forward pastors who were prayed over by the congregation. These pastors then blessed the businesspeople. It was a prayer of commissioning for scores who were dedicating themselves to be "marketplace ministers."

Jerry says, "The goal of Transformation Sunnyside is to bring substantial change through asset-based community development. The focus is on local assets, not local needs." Their aim is to encourage, develop, and demonstrate servant leadership that "empowers others to serve and succeed" in business, education, and in government.

Thanks to Ed Silvoso and his long-term involvement with revival in Argentina, Transformation Sunnyside also became a catalyst for prayer evangelism. Rosie and others prayer-walk the halls of most of the area public schools. Every week Christians pray at City Hall for the mayor and at the police station for the officers. At restaurants prayers are offered for the servers and the owners of the establishments. It is becoming commonplace for Christians to offer to pray for others in public settings.

While this prayer movement is bringing transformation to the community, it has transformed Jerry as well. His face lights up with an expression of delight and amazement. "What I discovered is that I can serve my employees by praying for them! I can evangelize on my own farm." He laughs, "I never knew evangelism could be so easy!"

Outward Focus

Although Jerry's lifelong arthritic disease, which has required replacement of two knees and one hip, has kept him from traveling to the "mission field," God used his medical condition to prepare him for a mission field in his own orchard and in his own hometown.

At the age of 20 the pain in Jerry's joints forced a choice upon him: would he become self-absorbed, or would he choose to focus his attention outside of himself? "To distract myself from the pain I decided to think about others." Rosie says that this decision shows in Jerry's life. "It made him walk slower, take a longer time, and build better and deeper relationships. He listens more instead of charging ahead, because his body can't keep moving at that pace." And then she says something beautiful. "It forced him to rest so that he could dream dreams to bless others. It forced him to be quiet and hear God's voice."

Jerry's arthritic "thorn in the flesh" has been a tool that God used to turn him outward, and the fruit of it can be seen all around: in the lives of his 70 employees blessed with an employer who is also their pastor, in thousands of Zambian families who are living better lives, and in a racially-divided, fragmented community that is being transformed.

As our visit comes to a close, Jerry sums up the ministry to which he and Rosie have dedicated their lives: "We want to see the perspective of Christians changed so they recognize that business is a gift of God, and that they are called to be servants who bless their employees and their community."

> "We want to see the perspective of Christians changed so they recognize that business is a gift of God, and that they are called to be servants who bless their employees and their community."

He then shares a private conviction: "The next spiritual revival will be among businesspeople who recognize that God has called and gifted them to be in business for the purpose of transforming their communities." Since they have both been exceedingly clear on the issue, had I pressed them I know they would have added, ". . . and the entire world—for Jesus' sake."

Zambia and North America: Reflections

by Doug Seebeck

Every organization tries many strategies early in its lifecycle. It was no different with Partners Worldwide. We had a reputation of always saying "yes!" to the ideas entrepreneurs proposed. If they were willing to take a risk, we were willing to stand with them.

But when Benedict came to us with his vision for Villages of Hope, we did some wrestling with him, and each other, because this was a unique venture. By that time we had determined that the most cost-effective way to create jobs was to work with international business organizations comprised of small- and medium-sized enterprises that were already in existence. Business to Business partnerships focus on what businesspeople do best—grow resources, create new services and products, provide new jobs, and build community. But Benedict's proposal did not fit that model.

Approximately 80% of all the active partnerships that Partners Worldwide facilitates fit the business-to-business partnership model, and about 20% are new innovations. Peter Neidecker, head of strategic planning for Hewlett Packard in Geneva and a partner with the Gitithia business group in Kenya, tells me that's not a bad ratio. If you aren't continuously innovating, you are not going to remain competitive. The trick is knowing how long to try a new prototype and, if it succeeds, how to develop and distribute the new product or replicate the new model.

So we wrestled with whether we should accept this innovative strategy that was outside of the business-to-business box. It was obvious that Benedict not only was a visionary, he was also an entrepreneur willing to take personal and financial risk. So we agreed to help him develop a self-sustaining orphan-care prototype with the goal of replicating the model in other places in Africa—especially where the numbers of children orphaned by HIV/AIDS were highest.

Benedict had learned from his first village in Namibia that caring for orphans is expensive. That experience also taught him the need to establish the model on the footing of economic sustainability. Because Africa still has abundant land resources, the Villages of Hope model has great potential for replication. It's also a sustainable approach for saving orphans with no extended family safety net while nurturing young entrepreneurs and building future leaders for Africa. Benedict is being strategically innovative, and he's onto something. Leaders of other countries in Africa have called to invite him to implement similar Villages of Hope in their countries.

In Chipata, the Farmer to Farmer program that Jerry Haak leads is also bearing remarkable fruit. The project has helped around 22,000 farm families and has successfully developed economic capacities that have moved them from food dependency to food security—and, in many cases, to food surplus. It's a low-profile project that is carried out by dozens of Zambian volunteers on bicycles. But because of the assistance of CRWRC, these families are being encouraged and empowered to provide care for more than 1,600 orphans. This is another wonderful model that shows great promise to address the AIDS orphan crisis where intact families are available.

I'll never forget the disappointment I heard in Jerry's voice when he called to tell me his doctor had informed him he had to cancel his trip to Zambia. He was deeply discouraged, but he quickly rebounded and phoned me just a few days later. "This is what I'm going to do," he told me in an upbeat voice. "I'm going to go to Gaston Point, Mississippi, instead and work with the Partners Worldwide team to develop a job-creation strategy for a community devastated by Katrina. I'll get someone else to take over my responsibilities in Zambia."

God used Jerry's trip to that town in southern Mississippi to let him see what years of institutional racism had done to block opportunity for the poor in his own country.

In February 2007, I was en route to Florida for a board meeting. I was heading to my airplane's departure gate when I met Jerry, who was en route from Gaston Point, heading for the same meeting. Now, Jerry is generally a happy and friendly kind of guy, but that day he was spitting mad. He described a shoulder-high wall that ran the length of the town to divide white and black neighborhoods. He was furious. Words poured out of him, describing historical injustice and the racism that still existed. But later, Jerry's righteous anger was transformed into a commitment to help bring healing to his community.

It would appear on the surface that Jerry Haak and Herm TeVelde, two white guys, were the founders of Transformation Sunnyside. That's what they thought, too, until Jerry met a Latino man named Roberto Matus and began explaining the vision to him. Jerry was surprised and elated when Roberto told him that he and other Latinos had been praying for just such a transformation for a long time. Specifically, they prayed that the Lord would move in the hearts of their Anglo brothers and sisters and that he would heal the racism and division in their community.

Jerry also learned that Roberto was a trainer in Servant Leadership, having gone through the Training for Trainers course in the Center for Sharing founded by Jerry's mentor, Cheryl Broetje. Soon afterwards, this Latino prayer warrior became one of the leaders in the Transformation Sunnyside movement.

Cheryl and Ralph are living and leading perhaps the most important strategic piece of our partnership model: the priority of advocacy. Just as Christ advocated for us, the Broetjes advocate for foreigners and aliens, taking to heart explicit commands God laid out in his Word. Ralph and Cheryl are modeling for us faithful obedience to an important duty we want to learn to take more seriously.

Creating a level economic playing field through advocacy is often the key to providing "access to the pond." Partners Worldwide members advocated for the Trade and Growth Opportunities Act for Africa, enacted during the Clinton administration. That Act created over 100,000 new jobs in textiles for Kenya, because for the first time Kenyans were able to export to the U.S. Similarly, when Partners Worldwide members advocated for legislation that forgave huge debt burdens accumulated in Africa during the Cold War, and rewarded those governments committed to reform, hundreds of thousands of children were able to go to school, new industries started, and jobs were created.

The Pew Hispanic Center estimated that as of March 2008 there were 11.9 million undocumented immigrants in the United States. The experience for most of them is what could be called schizophrenic: with one hand we welcome them to do the jobs most of our own people refuse, while with the other hand we threaten them. This is not how God commanded us to care for the alien in our midst.

Bob Naerebout, the director of the Idaho Dairymen's Association and a new Partners member, is painfully aware of how we are misusing the alien and how desperately broken our system is. Earlier this year Bob visited our office in Grand Rapids to ask for help in educating the church and our legislators about this domestic challenge that impacts tens of thousands of jobs and even more lives. We connected Bob with Cheryl and Jerry. Now, a small but growing group of partners who share the burden of undocumented immigrants and the biblical mandate to "care for the aliens and foreigners in our land" are committed to advocate with government leaders for these exploited members of our communities. Today, advocacy is a foundational component of the calling of Partners Worldwide.

Jerry and Rosie's journey, and the journey of all the other partners profiled in this book, illustrates dramatically the power of partnerships for reciprocal transformation. So many times I have heard our American partners say, "I don't know who is being helped more in this partnership—them or me. I don't feel like I'm doing very much compared to what I've received."

I think that is the mystery and beauty of what Jesus meant when he told his disciples that to gain their lives, they first had to lose them. By giving themselves away, they gained so much more.

While our North American partners may not have gained the entire world, they have gained dear brothers and sisters from new and far-off places they barely knew existed. They've found a new sense of purpose. They've experienced the blessing of knowing that their work has eternal consequences, and that God has called them to ministry in and through their businesses.

Making Your Business Your Mission

BY DOUG SEEBECK

I am writing this final chapter while reflecting on Partners Worldwide's international conference. "Business as Ministry 2008: Partnering to End Poverty" drew 310 participants from 24 countries and 26 states. Four themes leaped out at me at the conference—themes that have also been reinforced as we gathered and prepared the stories of the entrepreneurs profiled in this book.

1. God wants to bless the world he made.

Through his death and resurrection, Jesus Christ triumphed over *all* the works of the enemy, including poverty. Today, 854 million people in the world go to bed hungry every night. This is 12.5% of the world's population. While this is still a huge, unacceptable number, 30 years ago when I landed in Dhaka, Bangladesh, the percentage was 29%! Another way of measuring poverty is by the traditional dollar-a-day standard. Using that measure, about one billion people have grown out of poverty since 1980.

Yes, the last 30 years have seen an unprecedented upsurge in wealth creation and poverty reduction—more than at any other time in the history of mankind. For the first time, a majority of experts believe that we have the resources, technology, and ability to create a sustainable world with an absence of abject poverty. Economists, politicians, pastors, professors, and business leaders are beginning to see that such a world is within our grasp. We believe that God is raising up a new breed of missionaries in our day who will use business as a strategic means of extending God's kingdom in the world. The men and women you read about in this book are discovering that God wants to bless people of all nations and all economic situations. But what has brought them such unexpected joy is the revelation that God has uniquely gifted businesspeople just like them to carry out that blessing.

2. God works through relationships.

God chooses to partner with us, and he calls us to implement his mission by partnering with each other. But the reality is that partnerships are not easy, especially in crosscultural contexts. Each party comes to the table with different expectations, perspectives, cultural values, and priorities, so it takes time to truly understand each other.

At our recent conference, Pastor Oscar Muriu from Nairobi Chapel in Kenya helped us to read 1 Corinthians 12:14-27 through the lens of a world Christian:

> Now the body is not made up of one part but of many. If the American businessman should say, "Because I'm not African, I'm not part of

the body," he would not for that reason cease to be part of the body. And if the Canadian businessman should say, "Because I'm not Asian, I'm not part of the body," he would not cease to be part of the body. If the whole body were European, where would the sense of joy be? And if the whole body were African, where would the sense of order be? But, in fact, God has arranged all the parts of the body, every one of them, just as he wanted them to be. If they were all one part, where would the body be? As it is, there are many parts but one body. The Canadian businesswoman cannot say to the Latin American businesswoman, "I don't need you." Neither can the European businesswoman say to the South American businesswoman, "I don't need you." On the contrary, those parts of the body that seem to be weaker are indispensable, and the parts that we think are less honorable we treat with special honor.

The apostle Paul, who was from a culture that values relationships and family, was also a businessman. But when he described the relationship among Christians he did not use either the metaphors of the family or of business. Instead, he used the organic model of the body to suggest three key truths for successful partnerships, each of which have been displayed in the stories you've read:

- Partnership requires **interdependence**. No country, no business, and no person can say to the rest of the world, "I don't need you; I can go it alone." It is becoming more apparent than ever that we are in a global economy where no country is an island unto itself.
- Partnership requires **reciprocity**. No organ in the body is in a one-way relationship. Every part gives and every part receives. When parts of the body work at cross-purposes, they lose the energy-rich flow of love and the capacity to bear fruit for the glory of God.
- Partnership requires **mutual respect and humility**. As North Americans we especially need to humble ourselves and become learners before we try to make others understand us. We must learn the discipline of being slow to speak but quick to listen. We must enter partnerships with a commitment to elevate, to affirm, to bless, to acknowledge the strengths that our partners have.

3. We all have much to give and much to learn.

Francis Ssenyonjo, our Uganda partnership manager, summarized it best. Speaking about North American partners, he said, "One of the most helpful things they can do is just stand alongside and offer encouragement. They can provide such a great help by bringing a broader, larger perspective of business and of the world. They bring long-term thinking, strategic planning, a hopeful view of the future."

Based on his unique role bridging both the developing and developed world he made some helpful suggestions: "Those who come over should listen more and give us the opportunity to share openly. Only by quietly listening can they get an accurate vision of what is really needed. They should take the time to pray together with us so they can hear the Holy Spirit speak."

He continued, "North Americans tend not to value relationships as much. They value solutions. They like the quick fix. What our North American partners, especially those from the United States, need to know is that relationships are more valuable than money. If we all come to see ourselves as part of the body of Christ, as connected to each other spiritually, we will all have a greater sense of accountability for each other and for our relationship. If you and I see each other as members of Christ's body first, not just as businesspeople, we will know that we will not only have to give an account to him for material things but for how we treated each other."

4. Each one of us is called to become an agent of change.

We all have a vital and significant role to play in God's purposes for his creation. It is not by accident that you have read this book. God has an amazing vision for his world, and for you. His desire is to use you—with your unique gifts, abilities, personality, and experience—to help realize his master plan.

The apostle Paul has an intriguing term for change agents. He calls them "ambassadors." As a result of Christ's death and resurrection, Paul writes, a new creation has come, and it is manifested in reconciliation. God is reconciling us, and the whole world, to himself through Christ. As a result, we are also given the ministry of reconciliation as Christ's ambassadors. What has revolutionized the lives of the people profiled in this book is the realization that they can fulfill the calling to be ambassadors of reconciliation *in* and *through* their businesses.

God's plan is to have a world filled with his glory, where all his creation sees and acknowledges that he is gracious and merciful and worthy of praise. We have the privilege of partnering with our God and extending his reconciling work to every people group, community, and nation.

So whether you are a farmer or a food processor, a manufacturer or a merchant, a retailer, a raw materials expert, or the owner of a business, Jesus is calling you. He is saying to you, "Follow me, become an ambassador of reconciliation for me. You can do this, I am giving you my Spirit, and I will be with you until the end, so you have nothing to fear."

Partners Worldwide has a dream of a world without poverty because of a movement of businesspeople like you who understand they are called to business, and that their business is a place of ministry. I encourage you to join this movement of people who can say, "My business is my mission!"

Four Ways YOU Can Make a Difference

1. **Become a Partner**—Join the worldwide movement of business and professional people who are ending the cycle of poverty through the use of their skills and experience. Visit **www.partnersworldwide.org** for more information.

2. **Become a Financial Partner**—Commit to providing a financial gift to help create sustainable jobs for those living in poverty around the world.

3. **Become a Prayer Partner**—The most powerful weapon we have in our fight against poverty is prayer. Become an advocate for the poor through your prayers of encouragement and intercession.

4. **Share the book—grow the movement.** Give this book to your pastor, business associates, employees, customers, suppliers. For a discussion guide and additional resources, visit **www.mybusiness-mymission.com**.

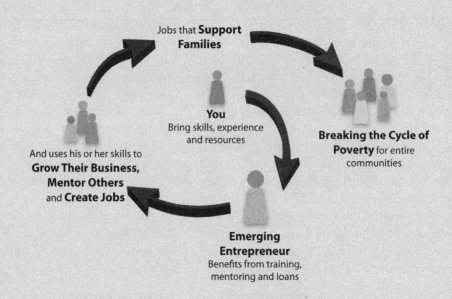

Jobs that **Support Families**

You
Bring skills, experience and resources

Breaking the Cycle of Poverty for entire communities

And uses his or her skills to **Grow Their Business, Mentor Others** and **Create Jobs**

Emerging Entrepreneur
Benefits from training, mentoring and loans

About Partners Worldwide

P artners Worldwide is an international movement of business and professional people following Christ by walking alongside the poor. They create and sustain jobs in developing countries by using members' business knowledge and resources to mentor, encourage, and equip businesspeople in these countries.

Arising in 1997 out of a need to confront unemployment in East Africa, Partners Worldwide has grown to serve in more than 20 developing countries around the globe. Partners Worldwide has established an international network of business and professional people dedicated to creating jobs, ending the cycle of poverty, and transforming communities.

The heart of their work is the relationships they forge. Through their global network, they link North American businesspeople with emerging entrepreneurs in Africa, Asia, Latin America and the Caribbean. Partnering together, they create innovative solutions for economic growth that restores hope and dignity to people around the world.

These combined efforts resulted in the creation of 1,656 sustainable jobs and the retention of 16,812 jobs in 2008. These jobs not only support families, but allow men and women to lift themselves out of poverty.

For more information, visit **www.partnersworldwide.org**.

Christian Businesspeople Transforming Lives

About Doug Seebeck

Doug Seebeck has provided strategic leadership as the Executive Director of Partners Worldwide since 1997. Before that, Doug served for 19 years with the Christian Reformed World Relief Committee in 12 countries throughout Asia and Africa.

Doug's passion for ending poverty through job creation and his extensive network of business and international development contacts has helped to fuel the growth of Partners Worldwide into 20 countries over the last 10 years.

Doug was born and raised in the Yakima Valley farming community in Washington state. He earned a bachelor's degree in agronomy from Washington State University and a master's degree in leadership studies from Azusa Pacific University in California.

Doug and his wife, Gail, have five children, and he dreams of a world without hunger and with employment for all by 2030.

About Timothy J. Stoner

Tim Stoner was born in Grand Rapids, Michigan, but he was raised in Chile where his parents served as missionaries. He spent his teen years in Spain. He earned a bachelor's degree in theology from Cedarville University and attended Grand Rapids Theological Seminary. He studied at Thomas M. Cooley Law School, earning a Juris Doctor in 1987. Since 1993 he has been in private practice specializing in estates and trusts.

In 1997 Tim published *The Paladins*, a fantasy/spiritual warfare allegory. *The God Who Smokes*, his first nonfiction book, was published by NavPress in 2008.

A few years ago, Tim and some friends founded Orphan Justice Mission, a nonprofit organization committed to caring for orphans by providing them with hope for a productive future. Currently, the ministry is helping a church in Uganda educate and feed more than 500 children, most of whom are AIDS orphans.

Tim and his wife, Patty, have five children, the youngest of which they adopted from Mozambique. They all live in Grand Rapids.

Acknowledgments

Over the past 30 years I have told countless colleagues and teammates who were wrestling with an important project, "If you can just imagine it, you can create it!"

I discovered it was much easier, however, to imagine this book than to create it and complete it. I write these acknowledgments with a heart full of joy, gratitude, appreciation, and love for the many people who helped make this incredible story come together.

I want to thank the scores of special people from communities in Bangladesh, Uganda, Kenya, Zambia, the Philippines, Haiti, Nicaragua, and the United States who helped inspire this book. Many are mentioned in this book, but there are countless others, however, who encouraged me to dream about telling these stories. You know who you are. Thank you from the bottom of my heart.

Gail, my wife and partner for the past 27 years, is a woman of incredible wisdom, strength, and beauty. People always tell me I "married up." I discovered that a book like this one is a labor of love, much of it from the author's spouse. The nights and weekends I owe her would take years to repay. Gail, thank you for your enduring love.

Tim Stoner has been an unbelievable partner in this project. I have been accused, at times, of being an intrepid risk-taker. I want to thank Tim for risking his law practice by dedicating six months to traveling to six countries on three continents—to see, touch, experience, and write about the lives of businesspeople on the front lines in the fight to end poverty. Tim was a tremendous encouragement to every person whose story is in this book, especially me.

I want to thank all the staff at Partners Worldwide for their patience, creativity, honest feedback, and hard work in helping ensure that we celebrated the dignity of the working poor and rich: the scores of entrepreneurs and businesspeople who are deeply blessed and who are blessing others. Special recognition goes to Roxanne Addink de Graaf for sharing her strategic mind and relational spirit in her outstanding work as project manager of this effort.

Our partnership with the Christian Reformed Church and the Christian Reformed World Relief Committee (CRWRC) is invaluable. I am especially grateful to their leadership and their staff for joining forces in a united attack on poverty. You are more than partners; you are friends.

Thanks also to Sandy Swartzentruber, our editor at Faith Alive; preliminary editor Catherine Cooper; and the dedicated reviewers who gave their time to help shape and sharpen this manuscript. Thank you for your technical expertise, your insights, and for caring about this project.

I want to offer a very special thanks to all the people in this book who shared their lives and their stories. I have the greatest respect and deepest admiration for each one of you. You are living testimony to the goodness in the world, and your lives inspire us all.

Finally, I want to thank you, our reader. Every dollar earned from this book is dedicated to the mission of Partners Worldwide: to encourage, equip, and connect businesspeople in partnerships that create sustainable jobs and transform lives.

—*Doug Seebeck*

I would like to express my gratitude to all those "missioneurs" who shared with me so generously and honestly—both those who are included in this book and those who are not. All your stories were powerful and encouraging. Meeting you has changed my life.

I also am so grateful to Partners Wordwide for affording me the privilege of visiting these quiet heroes scattered around the globe and telling their stories. This project has marked me indelibly.

And thanks, of course, to my wife, Patty, who put up with a husband who was away from home a lot and did so very graciously, believing that it would result in a book that would inspire and challenge many to follow Jesus boldly and serve him sacrificially.

—Tim Stoner

What People Are Saying About
My Business, My Mission

"Business as business we know. And missions as missions we know. But business as missions? From my first meeting with Doug Seebeck, I realized he was on the leading edge of 'BAM'—a breathtaking movement of God in the world's most needy marketplaces. In *My Business, My Mission*, Doug and his colleague Timothy Stoner have chronicled the amazing stories of pioneers on this emerging frontier. It is a landmark achievement!"

> —John D. Beckett, chairman of The Beckett Companies and
> author of *Loving Monday* and *Mastering Monday*

"Presented against the backdrop of God's love for the poor and within the context of sensitive crosscultural relationships, *My Business, My Mission* inspires and enables women and men with business skills to become agents of reconciliation who provide good news to the poor in Jesus' name."

> —Lynne Hybels, Advocate for Global Engagement,
> Willow Creek Community Church

"This is a transformational book that illustrates the power of the gospel of love. These are stories of modern-day disciples—businesspeople who are living out the ministry of economic, racial, and spiritual reconciliation to show what can happen when people are unleashed to be the body of Christ in the world."

> —Dr. John Perkins, founder of the Christian Community
> Development Association and the John M. Perkins
> Foundation for Reconciliation & Development

"This book gives me great hope about the future of Africa and that of the world. It powerfully illustrates the sacred trust that God has given businesspeople the world over: to develop and steward his resources, to nurture and sustain creation, to provide freedom from poverty through the creation of jobs and wealth."

> —Oscar Muriu, pastor of Nairobi Chapel, Kenya

"Be careful picking up this book, not because of its compelling challenge or intriguing stories. Be careful, because it might just get you wondering 'What if?' And that might end up getting you engaged in something that will have a huge impact on the lives of others . . . and yourself. This is clearly a dangerous book; put it down while you can!"

> —Rick Rusaw, senior pastor of Lifebridge Christian Church and author of
> *The Externally Focused Church* and *Living a Life on Loan*

"In *My Business, My Mission* Doug Seebeck and Timothy Stoner show us how to be the hands and feet of Jesus to the world. This is a must-read! You will be inspired, impacted, and catapulted to action through the true stories of real people who agreed to partner with those less fortunate to make a radical difference in their lives, in their families, and in the world."
—Phyllis H. Hendry, president and CEO, Lead Like Jesus

"As an ordained pastor and businessman, I am pleased to see this inspirational, compelling, and timely work. I strongly encourage pastors and businesspeople to read and reread this book. The partnership of business leaders and churches will transform lives and communities worldwide."
—Rev. Gerard Dykstra, executive director of the Christian Reformed Church in North America

"Entrepreneurship is not a lifestyle choice in poor countries—it is a matter of survival. The hunger for skills is vast. One of the central riddles in development is to provide business skills and connect entrepreneurs to networks. Partners Worldwide understands this critical fact and brings to bear the skill, commitment, and resources of entrepreneurs from North America and the global south in a powerful way. *My Business, My Mission* tells the story of a force to be reckoned with in international development."
—Dan Runde, former director of the Global Development Alliance initiative for the United States Agency for International Development

"*My Business, My Mission* tells the stories of men and women who experience business as an outstanding Christian calling and team up with creative, hard-working business builders in poor regions to make a long-term difference by growing human, business, and financial capital. The message that business can be mission will change lives and communities around the world."
—Gaylen J. Byker, president of Calvin College, Grand Rapids, Michigan

"Doug Seebeck and Timothy Stoner have done a masterful job of documenting stories of transformation as crosscultural partnerships are formed and business-people understand that they are anointed to use their business skills and talents to glorify God and extend his kingdom. These individuals and groups are pioneering the effort to help eliminate systemic poverty and restore to those in need the hope and dignity most of us take for granted. This is a challenging and inspirational book. Read it from cover to cover!"
—Ed Silvoso, author of *Transformation* and *Anointed for Business*